PRAISE FOR ÆTHER

"Meticulously researched, Baker's system of magical praxis stands on the shoulders of ancient wisdom, integrating Hermetic, Kabbalistic, Vedic, and Taoist principles. This will become your indispensable handbook of exercises.... An outstanding comprehensive monograph that I cannot praise highly enough."
—**BENEBELL WEN,** author of *The Tao of Craft* and *I Ching, The Oracle*

"Focusing on the practice of energetic working, the personal transformations that occur, and the spiritual hygiene required, this manual offers both an important perspective and a plethora of practical exercises to enhance and develop practice. This book is refreshing, invigorating, and long overdue!"
—**DAVID RANKINE,** esoteric researcher, magician, and author of many books, including *A Cunning Man's Grimoire*

"*Ætheric Magic* broadly explores various esoteric traditions to articulate a clear and practical definition of magical energy. This work is crucial because many alchemical methods become entangled in complex jargon, making them seem inaccessible and enigmatic. Baker presents these concepts of energy within a Western alchemical context that is straightforward and comprehensible."
—**NICK FARRELL,** author of *Helios Unbound*

"*Ætheric Magic* provides a rigorous examination of Western esoteric traditions, offering a comprehensive framework for engaging with subtle energies. The text meticulously explores a spectrum of techniques and practices derived from both historical and contemporary sources within the Western mystery and magickal traditions."
—**MAT AURYN,** author of *Psychic Witch, Mastering Magick,* and *The Psychic Art of Tarot*

"Drawing from some of the oldest extant textual traditions and well-established ceremonial systems of today, *Ætheric Magic* distills a much more coherent and practical system of what antique and Renaissance magicians considered the quintessential work of theurgy, referred to as *photagogia*—'invocation of the light.'"
—**JAIME PAUL LAMB,** author of *The Astrological Goetia*

"Baker's writing is clear and accessible. He offers a crisp summary of the structures underpinning both Western and Eastern magical systems and shows how they compare. The reader will discover how to develop, enhance, and control the magical senses needed to put aetheric magic into dynamic practice."
—**ISIDORA FORREST**, Senior Hermetic Adept and author of *Isis Magic*

"Baker elucidates the form and function of subtle energies and provides accessible exercises facilitating aetheric work. A comprehensive blend of theory and practice, *Ætheric Magic* is a valuable addition to every magician's bookshelf."
—**SOROR VELCHANES**, author of *The Planetary Magic Workbook*

"A masterful synthesis of Eastern and Western esoteric traditions. Baker has accomplished something truly remarkable here.... The book's exceptional organization and clear instructional approach make even complex energy work accessible to beginners while offering plenty of depth for advanced practitioners. This is a significant contribution to modern magical practice."
—**FRATER O.D.**, creator of *On the Mysteries* YouTube channel and Magick Circles

ÆTHERIC MAGIC

ABOUT THE AUTHOR

Ike Baker (Asheville, NC) is an author, content creator, practicing ceremonialist, and senior initiate of several lineages within the Western esoteric traditions, including the Martinist Order of America, Masonic Blue Lodge, and York Rite Freemasonry. He is also a temple chief of the Hermetic Order of the Golden Dawn. Ike is a traveling lecturer and instructor for multiple premiere educational organizations, including the Institute for Hermetic Studies. He has trained in Chinese herbalism and therapeutic body work, such as reiki and qigong. He hosts the *ARCANVM* YouTube channel and podcast, and he cohosts the *Aetherica Podcast* with Sky Mathis. Visit him at IkeBaker.com.

ÆTHERIC MAGIC

A COMPLETE SYSTEM OF

ELEMENTAL, CELESTIAL & ALCHEMICAL MAGIC

IKE BAKER

FOREWORD BY
IVO DOMINGUEZ JR.

LLEWELLYN
WOODBURY, MINNESOTA

First Edition
First Printing, 2025

Cover design by Shannon McKuhen
Interior art © Skyler Mathis
Interior art by the Llewellyn Art Department and Skyler Mathis on pages 36, 49, and 51
Interior art by the Llewellyn Art Department on page 42

Llewellyn Publications is a registered trademark of Llewellyn Worldwide Ltd.

Photography is used for illustrative purposes only. The persons depicted may not endorse or represent the book's subject.

Library of Congress Cataloging-in-Publication Data
Names: Baker, Ike, author.
Title: Ætheric magic : a complete system of elemental, celestial &
   alchemical magic / Ike Baker.
Other titles: Aetheric magic
Description: First edition. | Woodbury, Minnesota : Llewellyn Publications,
   [2025] | Includes bibliographical references. | Summary: "Uniting
   Western ceremonial traditions with Eastern energy healing practices,
   this book demystifies the æther and teaches you how to use it in your
   practice"— Provided by publisher.
Identifiers: LCCN 2024058953 (print) | LCCN 2024058954 (ebook) | ISBN
   9780738777818 (paperback) | ISBN 9780738777955 (ebook)
Subjects: LCSH: Magic. | Ether. | Alchemy.
Classification: LCC BF1611 .B275 2025 (print) | LCC BF1611 (ebook) | DDC
   133.4/3—dc23/eng/20250110
LC record available at https://lccn.loc.gov/2024058953
LC ebook record available at https://lccn.loc.gov/2024058954

Llewellyn Worldwide Ltd. does not participate in, endorse, or have any authority or responsibility concerning private business transactions between our authors and the public.
   All mail addressed to the author is forwarded, but the publisher cannot, unless specifically instructed by the author, give out an address or phone number.
   Any internet references contained in this work are current at publication time, but the publisher cannot guarantee that a specific location will continue to be maintained. Please refer to the publisher's website for links to authors' websites and other sources.

Llewellyn Publications
A Division of Llewellyn Worldwide Ltd.
2143 Wooddale Drive
Woodbury, MN 55125-2989
www.llewellyn.com

Printed in the United States of America

This book is dedicated to
Hermes Mercurius and the Universal Mercury.

ACKNOWLEDGMENTS

First and foremost, I would like to thank all my teachers past and present. Especially SND, RI, ECP, FQI, CL, and PL. Thanks also to Ivo Dominguez Jr., Heather Greene, Sky Mathis, and Ryan Sullivan for proofreading, editing, and submitting notes. Thank you to Benebell Wen for her insight, erudition, and kind generosity with her time in conversation. Thanks to my family for cultivating an environment where this kind of study and practice could be facilitated in its early stages. Special thanks to my partner, Nicole, for more than I can possibly list and without whom none of this would be a reality. Thank you to Luke for giving me a reason to get outside for a little bit each day during the most demanding stretches of this project.

CONTENTS

List of Exercises   xiii

Foreword by Ivo Dominguez Jr.   xv

Introduction   1

Chapter 1: Using the Ka   7

Chapter 2: An Alchemical Art   21

Chapter 3: Spiritus Animatus   33

Chapter 4: Mapping the Microcosm   41

Chapter 5: The Elemental Self   55

Chapter 6: Awakening the Æther   65

Chapter 7: Sound, Color, and Temperature   115

Chapter 8: Preliminary Techniques of Ætheric Magic   127

Chapter 9: Expanded Techniques   141

Chapter 10: Applied Techniques   163

Chapter 11: Developing a Practice   183

Conclusion   199

Appendix A: Glossary of Postures   201

Appendix B: Tables of Symbols   207

Glossary of Terms   213

Bibliography   219

EXERCISES

Chapter 6

Sky Gazing   70

Seeing Inward   71

Seeing Inward Variation   73

Seeing Inward Advanced Variation   73

Seeing Others   74

Feeling the Ætheric   75

Feeling Shapes   76

Feeling Shapes Variation   77

Feeling Energy Advanced   77

Scanning the Sphere of Sensation   80

Power Breathing   86

Breathing the Æther   88

Preparing the Middle Pillar Posture   90

Uniting Above and Below   92

Uniting Above and Below Variation   94

Three Centers Distillation   95

Control of the Sphere of Sensation   99

The Alembic   100

Harmonizing the Elements   101

The Elemental Circuits   104

Alchemical Circulations   107

The Macrocosmic Orbit   107

The Microcosmic Orbit   108

The Vortex   108

The Lightning Flash and Serpent   109

Charging the Points and Centers   111

Chapter 7

Sounding the Centers   117

The Tria Prima Power Centers   117

The Middle Pillar Spheres   118

The Universal Voice   120

A Symphony of Signatures   123

Chapter 8

Projection   129

Activating the Spheres   133

Invocation   136

Evocation   138

Chapter 9

Drawing an Invoking and Banishing Pentagram   142

Qabalistic Cross   144

The Calyx   150

Setting the Gates—A Warding Rite   151

An Exorcism of Water   155

Binding   157

Consecration   158

The Body Talisman Technique   161

Chapter 10

Hands-On Self-Care   163

The Crown Fountain   167

Personal Ætheric Defense   168

Entering the Underworld (a Pathworking)   171

Constructing Scrying Cards   176

Entering the Astral Gateway   177

Opening the Third Eye   178

Chapter 11

Ritual Bath   192

Ritual for a Venusian Talisman   193

FOREWORD

I first met Ike Baker by being a guest on his podcast *ARCANVM*. I've been on many podcasts, and I've found that there are very few interviewers who do a good job of bringing forth the central content and exploring the links to related ideas. Ike knows how to explore a topic and keep the dialogue interesting and productive. Later, I met him in person at a conference, and his enthusiasm and focus for learning and sharing knowledge were refreshing. In the time that I've known him, I have seen him take more interest in engaging with spiritual communities and systems outside of his starting point. It was inevitable that he would start writing books.

There is a shortage of books that offer clearly described methods and rituals for accessing and managing energy, especially ones that have a coherent framework to unify the techniques. The material in Ike's book *Ætheric Magic* is primarily rooted in Western ceremonial magic as well as alchemy and other paths, so he draws from a wide range of cultural sources and time periods. Sometimes admixtures of so many systems result in a clumsy assemblage with diminished applicability, but that is not the case in this book. There is a golden thread that runs through the material that brings order and utility to the various practices that are shared. Some potential readers may wonder whether this book requires extensive background in the Western Mysteries—it does not. Admittedly, I am a witch with a strong background in those systems, and as such I can verify that they are explained in a way that makes them more user-friendly. If you are a pagan, a witch, a polytheist, or some other type of practitioner, I believe you'll find that it contains unique and valuable resources that can be adapted and repurposed to fit your needs.

Ike has been an initiate of several Western esoteric traditions and is a Mason. He has been delving deeply into many forms of esotericism for about twenty years and has sought out the wisdom of many teachers. Ike's interest is more than intellectual: he applies what he has learned to his personal evolution and healing as well. Much of his work focuses on building bridges to connect practitioners, academics, and spiritual communities to adapt the best of the old so that it can grow in this time of great change. It is my hope that his book will open the way for newcomers as well as those who have lost faith in the possibilities offered by fresh connections between different systems of magic.

I suggest that you read this book slowly enough to truly make use of it. As you read the chapters, pause whenever something catches your attention, and think on how it relates to your practices, paradigms, and beliefs. After each chapter, summarize your insights and, if you are so inclined, jot down some notes. When there is an exercise, method, or ritual in the book, examine it closely and try to understand how and why it works before performing it. As you approach the end of the book, consider writing a ritual that uses some of these techniques but in your style or system. Books like this one are meant to be worked, and I believe this one has much to offer to those who do the work.

—Ivo Dominguez Jr.
    Author of *Practical Astrology for Witches and Pagans*

INTRODUCTION

In the esoteric schools of the East, there is a well-developed tradition of energy theory and cultivation, both in textual and practical format. In the traditions of Western esotericism, this is not necessarily the case. Some affirm that such a system does exist within the Western magical paradigm. However, it is obscured to the point of nonexistence in textual canons that don't reveal much about how the system works or how it can be developed within a Western magical paradigm. Some claim that the system of Western magical energetics is heavily veiled in order to keep this powerful secret out of the hands of potential abusers. More than ever, we have seen an explosion of interest in and practice of ceremonial magic, energy healing, and the occult arts. If indeed magic has penetrated the mainstream, then why not work in a direction that encourages a thorough and helpful understanding of the most basic and essential techniques and mechanisms of magic? Creating a system that enables universal accessibility and use of this force has been a personal passion project of mine for over a decade.

Throughout this work, I will introduce, explain, and expand upon exactly what ætheric energy is and how it is used. We'll examine its history throughout esoteric schools of thought both Eastern and Western, and we'll cultivate a well-developed theoretic model to effectively guide us in its safe usage. Finally, we'll begin to work with it in various stages. Our first question then is…

WHAT IS ENERGY?

Energy has been defined as the ability to do work. This tells us something about the nature of energy but not technically what it is. Einstein's famous equation for his special theory of relativity ($E=mc^2$) equates energy with mass, implying an important idea, namely that energy is vibration—movement—and movement requires something that can be moved. An example is found in kilocaloric or heat energy, which increases molecular rapidity, generating what we experience as heat. In reality, we cannot thoroughly define energy as a substance, though we understand that it cannot be destroyed, merely transformed, as is stated in the first law of thermodynamics and the scientific principle of the conservation of energy. For our purposes, we will define energy as *the basic unit of the union of force and form.* Energy in this case is more a phenomenon than a substance, but it utilizes matter, inducing it to motion. In the case of potential energy, there is a buildup and storage of potential for this phenomenon to occur. For many years, there was a theory posited by various scientists, including its founder Heinrich Hertz (1857–1894) and Nikola Tesla (1856–1943), that explained the many forms of energy (e.g., electricity, light, sound, etc.). It was by way of an all-permeating substance or substrate in and through which these various phenomena moved. This was called the *æther.*

THE ÆTHER

This brings us to our next question: "What is the æther?" Anticipating this scientific idea in his dialogue *Cratylus*, Plato writes, "[Air] is called *aêr* because it raises things from the earth, or because it is always flowing, or because wind arises from its flow?... As for aether, I'd explain it as follows: it is right to call it *aeitheer, because it is always running and flowing about the air.*"[1]

This substance of æther was also recognized in the yogic traditions of ancient India, where it was referred to as *akasa.* Akasa was conceptualized as the substance that facilitates the expression of the other tattvas or elements. Rama Prasad wrote in his classic introduction to the elements of Vedic cosmology known as the *tattvas* entitled *Nature's Finer Forces*, "It is out of Akasha that every form comes, and it is in Akasha that every form lives. The Akasha is full of forms in their potential state."[2]

In this sense, it can be conceptualized as a field or the basic energetic substrate through which all forms of energy manifest themselves. It is changeable and able to be conditioned into a specific state from a non-specific or latent state. Certain specific, latent qualities can be drawn forth from it to expression. The Florentine Renaissance translator and polymath Marsilio Ficino, who translated the *Corpus Hermeticum* and the works of Plato and the Neoplatonists, described the æther as the "quintessence," or

---

1. Plato, *Cratylus*, in *The Complete Works of Plato*, ed. John M. Cooper (Indianapolis: Hackett Publishing, 1997), 128.

2. Rama Prasad, *Nature's Finer Forces* (Adyar, India: Theosophical Publishing House, 1947), 23.

fifth element. He also referred to it as "spirit" and spoke of its "fiery and starry nature."[3] Ficino conceived of this energy as a kind of celestial body that served as an intermediary between the physical body of a thing and the higher realms that transcend physical manifestation.

There are many names for this energy; however, I've found it helpful to standardize certain terms for ease of comprehension and communication. *Æther* will be used throughout this book to refer to this subtle life force energy that animates, permeates, and exists within and without the physical body. This energy can be cultivated and directed, but in most cases, specific things must first take place before this can happen. I'll share these and how to intentionally self-catalyze and develop them throughout the course of this book.

The third question is "How do we know what the æther is?" The answer to this spans millennia of human history. From the earliest extant historical texts and artwork, we find evidence of a tradition of natural magic that embodies a metaphysics and practical application recorded in images and symbols. We are left to decode these symbols, since for most of human history, there was no standardized scientific vernacular with which to communicate these curiously hidden natural laws. I'll be sharing some of the historical documentation in order to contextualize and deepen our understanding of the æther and how it can be used.

Why and How?

The fourth question is "Why is this important?" Let's use the analogy of driving a car. Does someone who drives a car *need* to know anything about cars in order to drive one? Perhaps a few superficial details, such as the difference between automatic and manual transmissions and how to change a tire in case of a flat, but that knowledge doesn't necessarily make someone a great driver. What if they knew a bit more about the machinery—the technology—upon which they rely? This deeper level of knowledge might assist them in selecting the best possible vehicle for their needs, in turn getting them to their destination by the most direct path, saving time and energy. What we're talking about are power and efficiency. Further, what if the driver wanted to make modifications to the vehicle to customize their drive-time experience to the contours of their daily routes and needs? What if they needed to make a technical alteration on the fly or

---

3. Ficino, Marsilio, *Three Books on Life*, bk. 3, ed. and trans. Carol V. Kaske and John R. Clark (Binghamton, NY: Medieval & Renaissance Texts & Studies and the Renaissance Society of America, 1989), 535.

contribute some meaningful innovation to the field? They would need to have a deeper understanding and working knowledge of these mechanisms in order to achieve any of this. It's the same with magic. We can't go wrong becoming more intimately acquainted with the forces we utilize and work with so deeply in our magical practices, which are to us a spiritual technology.

The last question we inevitably arrive at is "Okay, so how do we use it?" Throughout magical literature as well as in practice, there are several stages or initiations that must take place before we can fully utilize and interact with the ætheric energy in our own microcosms and in the external world, and we'll cover these in detail in the last two chapters of this book. Theory will be of great importance in our study and practice with the ætheric energy, because engaging with it has a renovating effect upon our lives. We begin to truly work with and change our own energetic signatures, and with that often comes (to a greater or lesser degree) a somewhat disruptive life experience. Yet this is an inevitable part of the work, and to omit this caveat would be to lead people into difficult territory without necessary precaution, which would be unethical and karmically foolish. Therefore, we'll also discuss ways to mitigate these risks and hone further development and control of our personal ætheric energy.

EAST AND WEST

In the early 2000s, after taking an interest in comparative religions, I was inevitably led to study both Western and Eastern esotericism, eventually being initiated into a tradition of Western ceremonial magic as well as an Eastern modality of energy healing. The initiations took place within a week of each other. As time went on and I ventured deeper into these traditions, certain unavoidable similarities began presenting themselves with increasing significance. Over time, I began to understand each system as a particular expression of one holistic reality—both sides of a single coin. These similarities are striking evidence of a single underlying philosophy of being and magic and are summed up as concisely as possible as follows:

- Every created thing is a miniature universe—within every possible permutation of being are the qualities of the elements and of the stars.
- The elemental aspects of a thing are present in its constituent physical (and when reflected in an individual, psychological) makeup. The quintessential or ætheric aspect is a less tangible yet vitalizing or animating aspect of its being.

- Physical and spiritual changes can be made by a practitioner by conscious use and direction of these forces, most especially the ætheric force.
- The ætheric force is a real and tangible thing that can be sensed by one or more of the physical senses.
- The command centers from which these changes may be caused to take place are the mind and heart of the practitioner.
- This ætheric force is the source of much of what we call magic.

In both the Eastern and Western traditions in which I was initiated, this force had many names: *qi*, *ki*, *prana*, *ruach*, *azoth*, *light*, and more, but all these refer to a common concept: a field of energy within and surrounding all things that supports and maintains their vitality—a life force. It can be the source of either health or illness as well as have influence and be influenced by mental-emotional states. It receives impressions just as it imparts the same to the physical organism. It can be made to travel beyond its normal bounds, having influence and action at a distance, and it can be drawn forth from one source to be fixed within another material object or space.

HOW TO USE THIS BOOK

In my own estimation, the knowledge and conscious, intentional use of this energy is one of the most important factors of a successful and powerful magical practice, as well as in the general health and well-being of a practitioner. In the following pages, I'll present historical evidence that not only will inform our practice on the level of knowledge base but will also give tremendous glimpses of how this energy is controlled and directed. We'll also trace its roots and emergence in Western esoteric traditions, which are the foundations upon which all modern forms of magic are built. The exciting thing is that I won't be reducing all this to a mere history lesson! I'll also be reviewing time-tested theoretical models and practical applications of learning to sense this energy, bring it under conscious control, and cultivate and direct it toward magical ends via ritual, breath work, movements, and visualization techniques and exercises. The layout could be conceptualized as having three parts: history, theory, and practice. This work is essentially a preliminary manual for what I call ætheric magic. It's not necessary that the practitioner be entirely acquainted with the history before getting started. You don't have to read the book in any particular order. In fact, I encourage you to read and work whatever section of this book you feel called to. However, it is recommended that the theory at least be somewhat understood before beginning the practical exercises.

As a manual, this work also lays out a complete praxis of ætheric magic that can be worked as a stand-alone system. However, a practitioner can further use this manual as a tool to support and deepen their current understanding of different types of magic, incorporating whatever techniques they find useful into their existing practice. One might even go so far as to begin designing custom rituals with these techniques and exercises as a foundational basis. Some of the techniques given in this book may be somewhat familiar to experienced practitioners, but the development of ætheric senses, finely honed skill in moving energy, and the conceptual map of the practitioner's ætheric field are innovations to established systems that serve to seriously amplify healing, intuition, personal power, and magic. This synthesis of ritual praxis, visualization, and energy work transforms our magic from something that we do to something that we embody.

With all this said, let's move on to our investigation of ætheric energy, starting with one of the most significant ancestors of the Western magical traditions: ancient Egypt.

CHAPTER 1
USING THE KA

Magic is a force so powerful that the ancient Egyptians deified it in the form of Heka, the god of magic. Heka was so significant that he was very often included in hieroglyphic depictions among the deities that sailed on the solar boat of the Sun god Ra, upon which they sailed through the heavens by day and the underworld by night. To the Egyptians, the inclusion of Heka—magic—among this august entourage signified that he was indispensable to the generation and maintenance of all creation.

THE KA

In the ancient Egyptian worldview, physics and metaphysics were inseparable; they were two parts of one whole. Spiritual principles abounded throughout the manifestation of material things, animating them by certain hidden, or "occult," powers. It was among the chief duties of the Egyptian priest-class to discover these interior, hidden mechanisms, one such being Heka. From their investigations, the ancient Egyptian priests came to conceptualize an individual as consisting of at least nine aspects, ranging from most physical to most spiritual.[4] These were:

1. **Khet: The body.** This was the physical body.
2. **Ren: The name.** This was the personal identity of a being and the key of their essence, or blueprint, so to speak.
3. **Ba: The soul.** This was the spiritual vehicle of the personality of the individual and separated out to higher realms after physical death. The Ba was the part of the spiritual architecture of an individual that could travel between the worlds, so to speak, and this was illustrated by its hieroglyphic symbol, a bird with a human head. The Ba was intimately linked to the Ka.

---

4. Rosalie David, *Religion and Magic in Ancient Egypt* (London: Penguin Books, 2002), 116.

4. **Ka: The life force.** Also called the "vital essence" of a person, this was the animating force that kept them alive. It also had the potential to continue on after death and was symbolized hieroglyphically by two hands upraised at right angles to each other or by an identical (sometimes miniature) copy of a person—a kind of twin. The Ka was conceptualized as being a "double" of the physical body in that it took on the same shape.

5. **Khaibit: The shadow.** This aspect of a person was intimately tied in some sense to their actual physical shadow, but it also was understood to be an essential part of a person, since it went everywhere they went in life. Sometimes statues of people and deities were also called a *Khaibit* or *Shuyet*.

6. **Jeb: The heart.** The heart was considered an important and sacred organ to the ancient Egyptians. It was the seat of consciousness and conscience and would be weighed in the afterlife against the feather of *Ma'at*—or Truth—to determine a soul's fate.

7. **Akh: The immortality.** This corresponded to what many would call the "divine spark." This was the aspect of the person that would travel on and dwell in the realm of the gods after physical death. For a time in ancient Egypt, it was believed that only the pharaoh had an Akh.

8. **Sahu: The judge.** This was a kind of incorruptible spiritual form that passed on to the eternal realms with the Akh.

9. **Sekhem: The power.** This was a very little understood aspect of the soul in modern times, but it can be conceptualized as the strength of will and the accumulation of power in a person to affect their own fate and the fate of those around them.

While all these parts of the individual's physical and spiritual makeup share in importance, our primary focus will be the *Ka*, or life force, because the Ka refers specifically to the ætheric vehicle.

In the Egyptian model, the Ka was a spirit-like "double" of a person that came into activity at an individual's birth and was essentially the energetic blueprint from and around which the physical organism of the dense body was formed and maintained. The Ka was also considered to be the root of certain deep-seated inclinations related to the instincts. This life force energy took the overall shape of the person and was their individual portion of the universal life force, which animates everything in the cosmos. The

Ka was nourished by the same sources the physical organism of the person was—food and drink. After physical death, the Ka separated from the body but still retained its own life. Oftentimes, it was encouraged to inhabit a statue in the likeness of the deceased. In fact, some statuary in the ancient empire was constructed specifically for this purpose. However, it did require offerings of food and drink to remain alive and, if given consistent access to these, could live on indefinitely. Much of ancient Egyptian mummification practice was to sustain the life of the Ka after the physical death of the pharaoh.

HUNGRY GHOSTS

Another fascinating record of this ætheric apparition is the Taoist folk tradition of "hungry ghosts." Emerging from esoteric Taoist cosmology and spreading to various regions of the Far East, the hungry ghost is thought to be the spirit or ghost of a person who died a traumatic death or lived severely unhappily in their lifetime. Typically, from beyond the grave, hungry ghosts are driven by intense desires, which their next of kin become responsible for placating by way of offerings. These spirits are thought to reside on the earth and do not die what is called the "second death"—the dissolution of their ghostly bodies.[5] They have been recorded in as many as thirty-six different categories and are a phenomenon widely attested throughout East Asian cultures.

The tradition of hungry ghosts in Japan was in part catalogued in a series of illustrated scrolls called the *Gaki Soshi*, depicting the suffering of these specters in their dismal afterlives. These are on display at the Kyoto National Museum.[6] Hungry ghosts have also been recorded as having a peculiarly specific effect on people with weak wills—hijacking or "possessing" their physical bodies, as well as those with weak physical dispositions, otherwise diagnosable in Chinese medical theory as "compromised qi" (pronounced *chee*). Hungry ghosts are also called *preta* in the Sanskrit of the Vedic traditions.

In the Taoist calendar, the seventh lunar month (around the time of August/September in the Western calendar) is the month of the festival of the Hungry Ghosts. At this time, it is believed that the "ghost gate" is opened to the world of the living, and that

---

5. Steven F. Teiser, *The Ghost Festival in Medieval China* (Princeton, NJ: Princeton University Press, 1988), 199.

6. "Tales of Hungry Ghosts (Gaki zōshi)," Kyoto National Museum, accessed August 29, 2024, https://www .kyohaku.go.jp/eng/collection/meihin/emaki/item03/.

hungry ghosts roam freely among us. Special food is prepared and offered to the ghosts on various altars and shrines.

It is impossible to have any meaningful discussion about hungry ghosts without also discussing the concept of qi. Rather than being an obscure, unscientific model, qi theory has been a major aspect in Chinese culture and Taoism especially. Esoteric Taoism and Chinese medicine rely heavily on the concept of qi as a subtle energy that flows through all things. This energy has a natural flow of movement and can be intentionally and consciously moved by humans. In acupuncture, this is done with needles. In qigong, this is done by certain breath work, visualizations, and movements. *Qi* itself means "life force energy," as well as "breath" or "vapor."

BEYOND KA AND QI

Qi has many comparable equivalents in other systems of energy work, as in the *pranayama* of Vedic yogic disciplines for instance. *Prana* also translates to both "life force energy" and "breath." Other concepts exist in Greek (*pneuma*), Latin (*spiritus*), Hebrew (*ruach*), and Japanese (*ki*) usage and textual traditions. However, it is the Vedic system of pranayama or breath/energy work that is the most well developed and preserved system of energy cultivation. The branch of yoga known as *kriya* yoga utilizes advanced pranayama, including complex techniques of rhythmic breathing and the direction of the breath in and out of specific orifices—exclusively left or right nostrils, for instance—attributed to the astronomical luminaries of the moon and sun, paired with visualizations in order to cultivate and purify personal energy and consciousness to the end of raising *kundalini*. Kundalini is the concentration of prana that resides at the base of the spine and must carefully be raised in order to awaken spiritual powers, culminating in illuminated awareness. A product of this kind of work is the development of special (magical) powers referred to as *siddhis* in the Vedic tradition.

THE LEVELS OF BEING

In order to develop a working theory of ætheric energy, we may look to the well-established model of the levels of being in Western occultism. This schema was imported from the esoteric yogic traditions of India and the Far East by the Theosophical Society in the late nineteenth and early twentieth centuries and was originally referred to alternately as the "planes" or the "bodies."[7] This model is a highly effective

---

7. Charles W. Leadbeater, *Man Visible and Invisible* (London: Theosophical Publishing House, 1964), 10–12.

construct, retaining frequent usage and widespread acceptance within the greater magical and esoteric communities to the current day.

The model of the levels of being is a stratified ontological hierarchy that describes the projection of spirit into material form. It can be viewed as a chain of consciousness in the broadest sense of the word, which is conditioned to varying degrees the further it descends from the source of being and the closer it gets to matter. Directional terms such as *descent* are somewhat arbitrary, but they help us better conceptualize this model as expressing a hierarchical chain of being from its source to the material form it inhabits. All things have this chain linking them to higher realities, as we see referred to time and again in magical and occult literature throughout the ages (Iamblichus, Agrippa, Ficino, et al.). As the soul descends into materiality, it takes on an existence (which we refer to as a body) in each of the planes it passes through, which become a part of the totality of their existence.

The levels of being have been delineated in as many as seven divisions of the spiritual architecture and physical organism of a person, presented from highest to lowest in hierarchical order.[8] I am utilizing a fourfold model in our system of ætheric magic, though many readers may be more familiar with the sevenfold model of the Theosophical Society, whose levels include the following:

1. **The Divine Plane:** The highest of all levels, which is to say that it is closest to monadic or unified conscious being.

2. **The Spiritual Plane:** The level of the individual soul, which is the purest undifferentiated self-consciousness a being can obtain while retaining a sense of individuality.

3. **The Buddhic Plane:** The level of pure consciousness and illumination. This plane represents the attainment of spiritual awareness that we find expressed in great religious leaders or awakened ones throughout history.

4. **The Causal Plane:** The level of abstract contemplation and the level of the higher self. This plane is also the level of manifestation of the great gods and goddesses of creation. This plane is associated with the idea of the higher mental plane (see below).

5. **The Mental Plane:** The level of the mind—that is, the level of thought. Though all the planes can be theoretically split into divisions of higher and

---

8. Leadbeater, *Man Visible and Invisible*, 20.

lower, the mental plane is often discussed in reference to this distinction. The lower mental plane usually refers to rational or dianoetic intellectual faculties and the level of personal ego, whereas the higher mental plane—here referred to as the causal plane—is a realm of abstract contemplation.

6. **The Astral Plane:** The level of the imaginal faculty; the eye of the mind. This level has a strong connection to the emotional life of a person and also the creative capacities of the mind, being directly adjacent to the mental plane. It is at this level that a magician may travel (in vision) through the planetary spheres and starry heavens.

7. **The Material Plane:** The level of physical existence in which human affairs take place. All the prior levels are condensed in the physical person like a container or anchor. The higher level of the material plane is the ætheric body or ætheric vehicle, whereas the lower level of the material plane is dense matter, which is itself inert or inanimate.

Of these, we will be focusing on the bottom three—the mental, astral, and material plane—with the inclusion of the ætheric as a sub-plane of both the astral and material planes, a connecting link. This diagrammatic form is merely for the sake of illustrative clarity. In reality, these aspects of the individual coexist and interpenetrate each other like an extremely fine web. I'll start with the most subtle or spiritual level and progress to the most dense or physical. Each of these levels possesses a higher and lower polarity within itself and blends into the others. It's important to remember that although each level is relatively distinct, they are all modifications of a single intelligent energy. Each successive plane is receptive to the plane "above" or preceding it and influential upon the plane "below" or succeeding it. We can think of it like different bodies of water. A stream will often lead into a river, and a river feeds into a larger body of water such as a lake. Water is continually flowing in a direction, leading from spring, to stream, to river, to lake with areas that are not easily defined as stream or river. Transitions in this flow blend into each other, not always delineating a clear and exact point of when river becomes lake, yet the direction of the flow is constant.

Again, in reality the primary spiritual energy that is the substratum of all the others is not vertically above but rather occurring first and emanating the others. The closest analogy we have to conceptualizing this extremely rarefied energy is to refer to it as light.

Higher Spiritual Plane/Body Lower
Higher Mental Plane/Body Lower
Higher Astral Plane/Body Lower
Higher Physical-Ætheric Plane/Body Lower

Planes and Bodies

The Spiritual Level

This level of a person exists in the most rarefied, "spiritual" plane. This is the aspect of the individual's spiritual architecture that is closest to divine unity and from which all the other levels of being emanate. This would correspond most closely in the Egyptian conception to the Akh.

The Mental Level

This level of a person exists in the realm or plane of mentation or abstract universal principles beyond time and space. This level corresponds to a person's higher, transcendent mental faculties, such as in the contemplation of abstract mathematics. It corresponds to the Sahu of the Egyptian model.

The Astral Level

This level of a person exists in the realm or plane of the mind's eye—the imaginal faculty. This is the realm of dreams, intuition, and creative inspiration. This is the individual's interface with the underlying blueprint of the material world. This corresponds to the Ba of the Egyptian model.

The Ætheric Level

Though not considered a discrete plane in its own right according to the sevenfold model, the ætheric was of extreme importance in eighteenth, nineteenth, and early twentieth century schools of magic. The ætheric level is the aspect of an individual's composite makeup that exists as a sublevel of the material. What does this mean? Again referring to the higher/lower relationship inherent to the mutable areas of these planes of existence, the ætheric level exists in both the lower astral level and the higher physical level. Being between the astral and physical levels, the ætheric is intimately subject to the influences of both.

The Material Level

Last, we have the physical level of an individual, which exists in the realm of the material but again partakes of the ætheric and, through it, is influenced by the astral. Since these levels emanate successively (from the top down, so to speak), it is impossible to operate in one level without the participation of any of the levels preceding it. It's like a kind of spiritual chain of command. Therefore, the ætheric body, composed of ætheric energy, is the animating life force of the physical. If it withdraws, the physical body will be rendered lifeless.

THE ÆTHERIC AND MAGIC

It is important to understand that the astral, material, and ætheric interpenetrate each other and possess areas of phase change as they flow from one to the other, similar to the way in which the signs of the zodiac flow into one another from cardinal to fixed to mutable. For example, we can analogize the ætheric plane in the following way. Let's say you are feeding fish in a fish tank. The area beneath the surface of the water can be likened to the astral plane. The area above the water can be likened to the physical plane. The area where the fish food rests floating on the surface, partly above and partly below it, can be likened to the ætheric plane. It partakes of both and links them yet is appreciable enough of a phase in the hierarchical chain of being to be considered its own body.

The ætheric can, for example, receive impressions from the astral and imprint those signals on the physical. Since the astral plane is the seat of the emotions, this influence is the way in which psychosomatic disease is considered to be generated in many forms of traditional and holistic medicine. Being of the nature of the physical—that is, existing in space and time—though extremely subtle, the ætheric body and ætheric energy are able to be perceived by the physical sense—for most, primarily by sight and touch.

A person in an unconscious state of awareness will be habitually receptive to all impressions on and of the ætheric level of their being. However, in a conscious awareness of this relationship through the cultivation of highly focused mental and emotional states, the practitioner can intentionally exert their will on the ætheric level, utilizing the chain of flow to which it is receptive.

This can, however, also take place unconsciously, as in, say, when the physical organism is subject to intense states of pain or pleasure or under any very intense emotional stimulus. In these cases, the ætheric body or a portion of it can be unconsciously molded and projected outside the body in various forms, to varying degrees. This accounts for much of the poltergeist activity occurring in houses where previous traumas have taken place. An effective magician's task is to consciously direct and control the quality, volume, and flow of their ætheric energy.

As we come full circle, there is an affirmation of all this in the word for magic in ancient Egypt—*heka*—which translates literally to "using the Ka."[9] Interestingly, the nineteenth-century French occultist and author Alphonse Louis Constant, known widely by his pseudonym Éliphas Lévi Zahed, frequently wrote about a magical agent or substance that he referred to as *azoth*. While typically vague and obscure in his writing, Lévi writes a particular passage in a small work entitled *The Science of Hermes* in which he explicitly tells us, "The secret agent of the magnum opus, the Azoth of the sages, the living and vivifying gold of the philosophers, the universal productive metallic agent is *magnetized electricity*, the first matter of the magnum opus."[10] The ætheric body corresponds to

---

9. Samantha Moenning, "Heka, the Ancient Egyptian God | Origin & Deification," Study.com, last modified December 27, 2022, study.com/academy/lesson/heka-egyptian-god-magic-medicine-origin-mythology-facts.html

10. Éliphas Lévi, *The Science of Hermes*, trans. Joseph Bouleur (Sequim, WA: Holmes Publishing Group, 2007), 10.

the Ka, and it is this level of being with which we are primarily concerned in ætheric magic.

While we understand ætheric energy to be its own form of subtle energy, the tactile sensation of it is one of both static electricity and a kind of magnetism, which makes limbs feel as if they are being pulled in certain directions by an invisible magnetic force. In its visual perception, it can appear to be a radiant, static-like sparkle, like tiny sparks, which move in what oftentimes appear to be fluid-like currents.

In short, the level of the ætheric is the receptacle and connecting link between the inner or higher realms and the physical body. Together with the physical and astral levels, the ætheric composes one third of the magical triad. This somewhat mysterious force is attested in nearly every major tradition of antiquity for which we have a historical record.

The Aura

This brings me to an important consideration that may have already been nagging the reader: What about the aura? In the ancient Egyptian model, the Ba and Ka were considered a kind of pair. The Ka resided within the Ba, which was the aspect of the spiritual body with the capability of traveling between the worlds of the material and the Duat—the underworld. The Ba was capable of ascending to higher realms but frequently lived on in the material realm after death and required the nourishment of physical offerings for its continued existence here. The Ba can be conceptualized as the microcosmic ovoid of the aura, sometimes referred to as the *merkaba,* a term referring to an ancient form of Hebrew chariot mysticism. In this system, dating to the first few centuries CE, ancient rabbinical practitioners formed a vehicle referred to as a chariot (merkaba) within which to travel through the planetary spheres in a spiritually theurgic act of cosmic ascent.

There is a well-established Vedic tradition that deals with the aura, and it is this tradition that is the source of much of the widely accepted information about the aura among Western occult and spiritual communities. Much of this information was imported and reinterpreted by the Theosophical Society of the late nineteenth and early twentieth centuries. In the ancient theurgic traditions of Neoplatonism, the aura was referred to as the *augoeides.* This term is often translated as "radiant body" because of the way in which it is described in ancient Neoplatonic theurgic texts as being radiant or shining.[11] The Greek word *auge* translates to "shining" or "radiant."

---

11. Porphyry of Tyre, *Select Works of Porphyry* (Gloucestershire, UK: The Prometheus Trust, 1999), 145–67.

The aura is composed of ætheric energy and represents the outermost boundary of the personal microcosm, or "little universe."[12] Part of our training in the system of ætheric magic will be learning to see and feel the auras of others, as well as controlling and manipulating certain aspects of our own. For our purposes, we will refer to the aura as the *sphere of sensation*.

USING ÆTHERIC ENERGY

The ancient theurgists, such as Iamblichus and others, spoke of the utilization of this force or light. The technique of purifying the luminous body and drawing down divinizing light into it, by which the practitioner could encounter and have affinity to the gods and goddesses, was called *phōtagōgia*. In theurgic philosophy, this light was thought to emanate in and throughout the æther. It can act upon the *okhêma pneumatikón*, or spiritual vehicle of the theurgist, imparting various virtues and supranatural powers.

The cultivation of ætheric energy is one of the most potent and effective sources of power available to a person. In itself, it is neutral until a practitioner directs it to a specific purpose. This is why so many practical occultists and mystics have continually warned that this power has the potential to heal or destroy. If a practitioner doesn't exercise due caution and work from their heart, the ends to which this energy can be directed may be disastrous, to put it lightly. Ætheric energy is powerful in that it acts similarly to a fuel source; it is the generative force that empowers a ritual toward specific ends. The other forces at play in this magical symphony—the astral and mental—largely rely on the ætheric as the generative force for the manifestation of an intention; therefore, ætheric energy can be viewed as our creative potency. In this sense, it is strongly linked to a practitioner's libido, in that the sexual urge, from a biological perspective, is primarily a creative one. The accumulation of ætheric energy will therefore raise the sex drive of the practitioner, which can cause intrusive thoughts and physical discomfort. When ætheric energy is intentionally cultivated and consciously controlled by the practitioner, blockages and excessive accumulations can be sensed and balanced. If the practitioner cultivates ætheric energy without remaining cognizant of what is happening in regard to their sex drive, they may be driven toward reckless and impulsive ends. Sublimation, a technique utilizing sexual energies for other creative endeavors such as painting, writing music, exercising, and so on, is an age-old technique. While sometimes presenting to modern people as more of a moralistic or prudish finger wagging, lore regarding

---

12. Arthur Edward Powell, *The Etheric Double: The Heath Aura of Man* (Wheaton, IL: Quest Books, 1969), 3.

the accumulation of ætheric energy consistently tells of the derangement of the practitioner when this caveat is not well-heeded. I should also point out that there seems to be a direct correlation between an increase of this energy with the waxing and full phases of the lunar cycle.

Finally, I should stop and clarify some terminology. There is a great deal of confusion in the literature dealing with the ætheric body and ætheric energy, as it seems to have been referred to in the past as both "etheric" and "astral." For clarification, I'll share this quotation by the Theosophist A. E. Powell: "In early Theosophical literature it was often called the astral body, the astral man, or the Linga Sharira. In all later writings, however, none of these terms are ever applied to the Etheric Double … not to confuse the two quite distinct bodies, known to-day as the Etheric Double and the Astral Body."[13]

While the Theosophists Annie Besant and C. W. Leadbeater, who effectively took control of the Theosophical Society after Helena Blavatsky's death, are typically cited as the source of this change in nomenclature, instances of this particular confusion can be traced as far back as ancient Greek philosophy. In Plato's works, he refers to the celestial quality of the human soul, and from this we derive the term *astral*, meaning "of the stars."[14]

As mentioned earlier, the astral level in our system of classification is accessed by a practitioner's imaginal faculty—the eye of the mind—whereas the ætheric is an extremely subtle physical substance, able to be observed and sensed, and the energy of the ætheric body can be molded and projected outside the physical body. Some techniques utilizing a method of projecting the practitioner's consciousness to this exteriorized ætheric form, also referred to as a simulacrum or a body of light, are similar to the well-documented occult practice called astral projection. The technique of projection of ætheric energy can be used in several ways magically. An example of this is in talismanic charging and consecration techniques utilized by the Hermetic Order of the Golden Dawn and the Taoist *fulu* traditions, which we will discuss in the following chapter. It can also be used to formulate and empower other magical images, such as deity forms or astral-ætheric images worn by the practitioner like a garment as an attenuated form of invocation and the embodiment of specific deific powers in a consecration ceremony or other ritual, such as initiation, for instance. The techniques employed using the power

---

13. Powell, *The Etheric Double*, 2.

14. Plato, *The Timaeus of Plato*, trans. R. D. Archer-Hind (New York: MacMillan & Co., 1888), 142.

of the ætheric can evolve the amplitude and effectiveness of any particular working by several orders of magnitude.

CONCLUSION

The ætheric body has long been studied by ancient cultures east and west and is conceived as an aspect of the spectrum of being that comprises the totality of an individual person—physically and metaphysically. It has been referred to by many names, and there are still extant traditions codifying its nature and use. Æther, and the ætheric body itself, was thought to be an essential mechanism of magic by the ancient Egyptians. By understanding its relationship to the physical and metaphysical components of creation, you can begin to sense and work with it in conscious, intentional ways.

CHAPTER 2
AN ALCHEMICAL ART

In both Eastern and Western traditional forms of magic, we find ample evidence of a force or power that can be summoned, accumulated, and directed. Astrological, and specifically talismanic magic, is perhaps one of the best examples of this. Astrological magic is a sophisticated branch of natural magic that can be used for any number of purposes—from mundane magic to spiritual theurgy. It has been compared and referred to in many traditions as a kind of clockwork of the universe. Ætheric energy is diffuse, meaning it permeates all things. Each physical object, whether an anatomical body or a coffee mug, has its own ætheric substrate (body/double).

Ætheric energy on the whole exists within the ætheric field, which is impressionable and awaits to be acted upon, particularly by the mind. In scientific vernacular, a field is an area in which each point is affected in some way by a force. Examples of fields are Earth's gravitational field, magnetic fields, and electric fields. The ætheric field can be manipulated by the practitioner after they have progressed through a course of development in cultivating a conscious awareness of and linkage with their ætheric body. I will be guiding you through exercises in this throughout the course of this book.

FULU TRADITIONS

In the fulu traditions of Taoist talismanic sigil magic, the *fu*, or sigil, is typically a composite symbol corresponding to modern Western sigil crafting.[15] Signs, symbols, characters, and words are enlisted for its crafting and are selected according to the force or forces intended to be invoked into it. In Taoist fulu ritual, the practitioner starts with a prayer to invoke heaven and establishes the Taoist cosmological trinity of heaven, earth, and human. This is typically followed by an evocation of the four guardians (*si shou*),

---

15. Benebell Wen, *The Tao of Craft: Fu Talismans and Casting Sigils in the Eastern Esoteric Tradition* (Berkeley, CA: North Atlantic Books, 2016), 33.

representing the four cardinal directions. This is then followed by an invocation of specific Taoist cosmological hierarchies, such as celestials, animal spirits, and both angelic and chthonic entities (in orthodox Taoist sigil craft).[16] Astrological and astronomical influences are of great significance for much of Taoist magic and cosmology, and the consecration or charging of the fu is no exception. After the invocation of the hierarchies comes the consecration of the fu sigil talisman.

In esoteric Taoist fulu and broader magical traditions, this is conceived of as an exchange of energy, specifically utilizing the giving, or dominant, hand of the practitioner as a directing channel. Wands are also used as extensions of this directing power. These techniques are performed in tandem with visualizations and breath work corresponding to the concentration of a force within the practitioner on inhalation and the outward projection of force on exhalation.

The fu itself is typically a composite symbol corresponding to modern Western sigil crafting. Signs, symbols, characters, and words are enlisted to craft a fu that is balanced harmoniously and appropriately according to the force or forces intended to be invoked into it, at which point it becomes a talisman.[17] This should be quite familiar to anyone who has performed a talismanic charging and consecration ritual before.

WESTERN MAGIC AND CARDINAL DIRECTIONS

Western magic is predicated on nearly identical elements, protocols, and procedures. In a traditional Western talismanic ritual, there would be an invocation, perhaps of the Four Archangels. Ceremonial magicians familiar with the Golden Dawn will find this in the Rituals of the Pentagram for instance, with the invocation of Raphael, Michael, Gabriel, and Uriel. In its original iteration, while also calling to mind corresponding elemental attributions, the Rituals of the Pentagram are actually directional rituals, as the elemental "dispositions" of the quarters are directly corresponded to the four winds (i.e., easterly, southerly, westerly, and northerly).[18] In other words, the cardinal directions are the rationale for the elemental attributions. This can also be found in other warding rites, such as the Setting of the Wards of the Ordo Aurum Solis, the aforementioned Taoist consecration ceremonies, and circle casting in Wicca.

---

16. Wen, *The Tao of Craft*, 146–47.

17. Wen, *The Tao of Craft*, 107.

18. Samuel Scarborough, "The Lesser Ritual of the Pentagram," in *The Light Extended: A Journal of the Golden Dawn*, vol. 1, ed. Frater Yechidah (Dublin: Kerubim Press, 2019), 59.

The Four Cardinal Directions				
Direction	Element	Qualities	Wind	Archangel
East	Air	Hot and Moist	Euros	Raphael
South	Fire	Hot and Dry	Notos	Michael
West	Water	Cold and Moist	Zephyros	Gabriel
North	Earth	Cold and Dry	Boreas	Uriel

CHAIN OF FLOW

Magical invocations of particular metaphysical hierarchies are most often based on the "chain of flow" set forth in Heinrich Cornelius Agrippa's *Three Books of Occult Philosophy,* which are based on the Neoplatonic ontological hierarchies as organized by Pseudo-Dionysius in the fifth century CE. These hierarchies are important to the practice of magic because they compose a workable model of the chain of being. It was conceived in traditional magic of the East and West that this great chain was what connected everything, that it was the direction of flow of all creation from the highest deity to the smallest particle of matter. As Agrippa put it, "All inferiors are governed by their superiors."[19]

You saw this in the discussion of the chain of flow of the planes and bodies of Theosophy. Magicians of earlier ages discovered that this descending direction of flow could be utilized similarly to the way in which waterways were used to generate power. Appropriate channels could be selected, and a very particular type of influence could be diverted for a specific kind of use. These early magi also discovered that the chain of being could be traversed by the practitioner in the opposite direction; it could be used like a ladder to the heavens. This mode of traveling the hierarchies back upward toward divine realms was the theoretical model of ancient theurgy, or "god-working."[20] This interplay and exchange of particular energies is important in ætheric magic, as it constitutes a method of invoking and working with specific energies within our spheres of

---

19. Heinrich Cornelius Agrippa, *Three Books of Occult Philosophy*, bk. 1, trans. Eric Purdue (Rochester, VT: Inner Traditions, 2021), 16.

20. Gregory Shaw, *Theurgy and the Soul: The Neoplatonism of Iamblichus*, 2nd ed. (Kettering, OH: Angelico Press, 2014), 5–6.

sensation, which as mentioned earlier is a Western term for the broader psyche-ætheric architecture, including the aura, of the practitioner.

SPIRIT OR FORCE?

At this point, a question of terminology should be addressed. Magicians familiar with these hierarchies, which comprise a great deal of astrological magic, may be confused in referring to these as energies or forces rather than spirits and intelligences. The question has long been posited by magicians and occultists: Are these energies or spirits we're working with? Ultimately, consciousness is a kind of energy that, as we know, can neither be created nor destroyed. It is this self-aware capacity of human beings that allows us to be able to consciously direct these energies, using specific words, symbols, gestures, and visualizations. In the esoteric worldview, as in forms of panentheism, all things contain differing degrees of consciousness. So we could very easily conceptualize these as both—energy and consciousness.

Interacting with these forces as if they were autonomous, self-reflective entities has tremendous advantages, but the key to the resolution of this issue of terminology is in the conceptual model of the microcosm and macrocosm. This idea was put forth in its earliest stages in the Platonic dialogues, specifically the *Timaeus*. It views the individual human as a miniature universe, existing within and composed of the essential constituents of the great universe, the physical boundaries of which are delineated by the outermost ovoid of the sphere of sensation. A popular phrase that expresses this in magic and occultism is "As above, so below," taken from the Emerald Tablet of Hermes Trismegistus. Each objective manifestation of nature and the greater cosmos has a corresponding subjective aspect within each one of us. Things like physical strength and energy as well as heat might fall under the correspondence of Mars. Things like imagination, dreams, and especially feminine bodily cycles would correspond to the moon. When we call with enough focus and emotion on a particular exterior manifestation of these essences (e.g., the planet Mars), we cultivate a predominance of the corresponding force within our microcosm which, when brought to its peak, diffuses itself throughout our sphere of sensation. We embody that force and become "charged" with it, so to speak. For that moment, we are as living talismans.

In many magical traditions, once a talisman has been charged, it is treated as a living being. This is not to say a spirit inhabits the talisman so much as the talisman has been charged or animated by a particular force or forces. In this sense, it is considered ensouled similar to the way in which the physical body of a person can be looked at as the talisman of its spirit or qi. These essences, which underlie all manifestation, are traditionally conceived of as thoughts in the mind of the Divine, and we as human beings partake of these through our own inherent divine natures and minds. In this way we are able to reflect and take part in the cosmic process of manifestation. When we enter into the magical state of mind and call down these intelligent forces, we also elevate our own consciousness, meeting them at a middle point. This middle point is where magic happens. From this magical point of balance, we can engage in a form of divine cocreation, beckoning these intelligent energies to conform to our magical intentions.

ALCHEMY

Another excellent example of energetic exchange in esoteric practice is in the art of alchemy. Alchemy is an art and science that was present at an extremely early time in the historical record of the East, particularly in China, and associated with Taoist esoteric practices. It is attested there in the first centuries BCE as both a physical science and as a spiritual practice.[21] In the Western historical record, modern alchemy first takes shape in the fourth, and fifth centuries BCE in and around the regions of Alexandria, Egypt, and the greater Mediterranean. It is in the writings of a Roman Egyptian scribe-priest and metallurgist known as Zosimos of Panopolis that we find it referred to as *cheirokmeta*, or "things made by hand." Zosimos is also the first to refer to the goal of alchemy as the philosopher's stone, and he described several allegorical processes that corresponded to the purification or evolution of the body and soul of a person in his alchemical texts.[22] In Taoism, this form of internal alchemy is known as *neidan*. Astrological placements were also extremely important in traditional forms of alchemy both East and West. Agrippa testifies that it is by the celestial bodies that we are able to grab hold of and direct universal forces.[23]

Alchemy has as its aim the cultivation of a state of perfection: the transmutation of base metals from lead to gold. The underlying theory behind this is that all things contain a divine part. Alchemy is almost a process of reverse engineering the physical—of going from a state of disorganized chaos to harmony. This state of harmony or perfection has

---

21. Shannon Grimes, *Becoming Gold: Zosimos of Panopolis and the Alchemical Arts in Roman Egypt* (Auckland: Rubedo Press, 2018), 135.

22. Grimes, *Becoming Gold*, 116–17.

23. Agrippa, *Three Books of Occult Philosophy*, I.16.

been given many different symbolic terms, such as the philosopher's stone, first by Zosimos of Panopolis in the third century CE.

From this stone was created the elixir of life. The perfected state has further been referred to as the quintessence. As noted earlier, this word means "fifth essence" and is related to the four philosophical elements: earth, water, air, and fire. The quintessence was thought to be an indwelling essence or substance that was present in all elements and their permutations. Therefore, it was considered to be within all things, yet remaining latent until purified by various techniques involving the activation and application of fire, water, and air. It is these techniques and their philosophical methodology that characterize the art of alchemy. It was through this process of reverse engineering matter through its constituent elements, following a specific set of protocols, that alchemists hoped to arrive at the production of the quintessence.

The essential formula that comprised these alchemical protocols was summed up by medieval and Renaissance alchemists in the Latin phrase *solve et coagula*—separate and recombine. This axiom alludes to the overall trajectory of a series of processes or stages in the alchemical work that is principally informed by Hermetic philosophy. These trajectories of intentional evolution, which make use of alchemical techniques applied both to the transmutation of physical substances and an individual's spiritual development, can traditionally be broken down into three, four, or seven stages. Generally, these techniques of gradual transmutation first act upon the ætheric and dense physical matter of the material to be transformed, ultimately distilling and strengthening the indwelling quintessence, which we may correlate to the perfected harmony of the physical and ætheric vehicles. They are as follows:

Threefold

Nigredo: Blackening
Albedo: Whitening
Rubedo: Reddening

Fourfold

Nigredo: Blackening
Albedo: Whitening
Citrinas: Yellowing
Rubedo: Reddening

Sevenfold

Calcination: Burning to ash

Dissolution: Dissolving

Separation: Filtration

Conjunction: Bringing together

Fermentation: Breaking down what has been conjoined

Distillation: Purification

Coagulation: Final solidification

There is also a twelvefold division of the alchemical stages, and this along with the divisions of four and seven stages will come into play later when we start to develop the theory of ætheric magical practice.

ALCHEMICAL DIVISIONS AND THE TETRAKTYS

The theoretical basis of alchemy has several other important interrelated divisions that constitute the underlying philosophy of its processes. We can find these summarized in the following diagram.

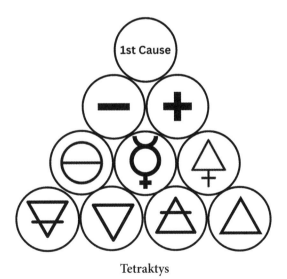

Tetraktys

As shown in the diagram, there is a numbered ordering of creative processes from the first cause to the generation of the elements. The permutation of the elements and philosophic essentials in alchemy is predicated upon the idea of an underlying unity that exists at the core of every single created thing. This is called the *monad*, from the Greek *mono*, meaning "single" or "one." The monad contains all subsequent possibilities and potentialities within itself and begins the sequence of generation by generating a *dyad*—a polarity—establishing the boundaries and parameters of further creation, as well as the spectrum between this polarity.

The polarity is often mentioned as masculine and feminine or positive and negative. I avoid gendered terms because these tend to obfuscate their essential, albeit archaic, meanings. Referring to polarity as positive and negative does not denote a value judgment but is more specifically like referring to the positive and negative poles of a battery—both are required and work together. The binary itself creates a spectrum of permutation by creating the space for potentialities of interaction and can be conceptualized most appropriately as active and receptive. In alchemy, we call these *celestial salt* and *celestial niter*, being the essences of receptivity and activity, respectively.

From the dyad, the *triad* is created. For anyone interested in the science of music, this can be compared to when two sonic notes are played in an interval. The vibrations of these notes or tones create a third tone, which is found to be in harmony or proportional ratio with two primary tones creating it, and is referred to as an overtone.

The triad formed by the dyad is the Tria Prima of alchemy; philosophical salt being the manifestation of celestial salt on a more dense plane, philosophical sulphur being the manifestation of celestial niter on the same, and philosophical mercury being the neutral or androgynous state that can be either or both—a combination of the energies of both states. It is important to note that we refer to these as "philosophical" salt, sulphur, and mercury because when we refer to them in this way, we are not referring to physical salt, sulphur, or mercury but rather to underlying states of being and matter, as generating material reality. The Tria Prima corresponds to the principles of body (salt), soul (sulfur), and spirit (mercury).

The Tria Prima expresses the four elements by a kind of governance. The quaternary model of elements (fire, air, water, and earth) was thought to be states or qualities of matter, each existing in a compound state with the others. Fire and air were thought to be rising, expansive, and volatile and so were considered the active elements. Water and earth were thought to be denser, sinking, heavy, and fixed, and therefore were considered the passive elements.

Sulfur, being the active philosophic essential, is conceptualized as governing the operations of the volatile elements of fire and air, while salt, being the fixed philosophic essential, governs the operations of the fixed elements of water and earth. Mercury, being the mediating, hermaphroditic philosophic essential, was thought to govern one of each polarity, (i.e., air and water). These elements then give us the qualities varying from dryness and heat to moistness and cold, as well as their permutations.

These philosophic essentials, being of a holographic and fractal nature, exist in everything as an underlying pattern of manifestation. When I say "holographic," I don't mean fake or illusory, but rather of the nature of a holographic image, which means that all the information of the image or thing itself as a whole is encoded into every part or aspect of that thing. This is essentially the doctrine of the macrocosm and microcosm. The four aspects or phases of the One Thing—monad, dyad of polarity, triad of the Tria Prima, and quaternary of the elements give us ten: the Tetraktys of the Pythagoreans. The left arm of the triangular Tetraktys contains the most passive aspect and the right arm contains the most active, with Mercury in the center as the mediating principle. This arrangement of the foundational essences of creation from unity to diversity also corresponds to the ten sephiroth of the Qabalistic Tree of Life. Familiarity with the Qabalistic Tree of Life overlain atop the physical body will work as a functional model of anchor points, correspondences, and types of energy and will come into play when you begin working with techniques of concentrating, moving, and selecting specific energies in your sphere of sensation.

SPIRIT AND THE SECRET FIRE

There is, however, one addition to the elemental aspects in alchemical theory: spirit—the fifth element or quintessence, which is considered as permeating the other four. This gives a fivefold system of the elements: earth, water, air, and fire, permeated by spirit. We find a fivefold elemental system also present in the ancient Taoist canons, though their system is slightly different. It consists of various stages and forms that matter takes, related to cycles of permutation. These include fire, earth, metal, water, and wood. Both Western and Eastern elemental systems are typically attributed to the angles of the lineal geometric figure of the pentagram, or five-pointed star. The elemental pentagram will be a significant diagram for our work with ætheric energy, as it exemplifies a sort of energetic circuit board. For all intents and purposes, we can equate ætheric energy generally with the element of spirit in the Western system of the elements, keeping in mind that it permeates the other four elements, binding them to each other and expressing itself through each. In the individual who has not learned to consciously direct this energy by a process of linking, this element of spirit remains largely diffuse and impressionable. This means that it will be moved unconsciously and is typically subject to certain accumulations and patterns that are not the result of conscious movement of it and can present issues to health and well-being, not to mention available power for ritual magic.

In Chinese medicine, qi (ætheric energy) can become blocked or move counter to its natural direction of flow, causing disease. It can also become weak or low in volume, or excess or disproportionately large in volume. All of these are etiological models within Chinese medical diagnosis. One of our preliminary goals will be to link this energy to conscious control. Before we become aware of and consciously direct our ætheric energy, we must undergo a process of physical and psycho-spiritual transmutation facilitated using the principles, symbols, and processes of the alchemical art.

Another alchemical concept of significance to our work is what the alchemists of old referred to as the "secret fire." Fire was a major component of alchemy, as the entire process was facilitated by varying degrees and applications of heat. The secret fire of the alchemists was thought to be extremely powerful—even miraculous—to the point that few could utilize it safely. Therefore, in many older alchemical manuscripts, it was symbolized by a sword or arrow. They also considered it the most difficult and prolonged part of the Work and referred to it as serpentine.[24]

In Eastern systems of energy theory such as in Traditional Chinese Medicine, this corresponds microcosmically to *jing*, or "essence." This essence is thought to be inherited from one's parents at birth and is responsible for overall physical vitality and transformation, such as that which occurs with aging and the body's metabolic processes. Its greatest concentration or source in the human body is located at a place within the lower abdomen, near the adrenals and between the kidneys. This corresponds to the Chinese medicine acupuncture point *mingmen*—gate of the fire of life. It is located on the spine at the second lumbar vertebra between the kidneys and is intimately related to the reproductive organs, being proximate to the ovaries in a female and just above the external genitalia, and therefore reproductive power. Jing is also intimately related

---

24. Dennis William Hauck, *The Complete Idiot's Guide to Alchemy: The Magic and Mystery of the Ancient Craft Revealed for Today* (New York: Penguin Books, 2008), 92.

to *yuan qi* ("source qi"), which is anatomically related to the kidneys and is the original substance that makes up everything in the universe.

These two can be thought of as an expression of kundalini in the yogic traditions. Kundalini itself is an extreme concentration of prana located at the base of the spine in the coccyx, believed to reside there in a latent state—coiled like a sleeping serpent. Kundalini is also related to primordial or cosmic energy. In specific types of yoga, kundalini energy is gradually raised up the central pillar of the spinal column. Of great importance to this operation is the speed at which it is raised. If not handled with patience and care, the flow of kundalini up the spine can be extremely painful and dangerous both physically and psycho-ætherically.

Our work of gradually becoming aware of and learning how to perceive ætheric energy will serve the end of an alchemical marriage. There is not one marriage but several, as these principles are holographic and fractal, as mentioned earlier. We also find a minor conjunction listed before ultimate coagulation in our alchemical stages. This initial conjunction, or lesser marriage of Sol and Luna, is the linking of our conscious mind (symbolized by Sol) to our latent, diffuse, and unawakened or receptive ætheric energy. Once this marriage of sun and moon (active and receptive) is accomplished, the result will be in an indissoluble bond—a new thing possessed of both qualities as a unified whole. This was represented alchemically by the *Rebis*, as well as Mercury, the divine androgyne and is often referred to as the "child of Conjunction."[25]

CONCLUSION

The work of ætheric magic is not merely theoretical or ritualistic but constitutes an alchemical transmutation of the self. In this process, you are the alchemist and the material being worked upon. The marriage of your conscious mind with your latent-receptive ætheric field is an alchemical conjunction of the active and passive, which results in a holism previously unattained. However, this is just the beginning of the work.

---

25. Hauck, *The Complete Idiot's Guide to Alchemy*, 235.

CHAPTER 3
SPIRITUS ANIMATUS

In addition to often being referred to as the *spiritus animatus*, or animating spirit, ætheric energy has also been referred to as animal magnetism in the work of the eighteenth- and nineteenth-century German physician Franz Anton Mesmer.[26] During an experimental phase of therapy involving the use of magnets, Mesmer claimed to have felt something akin to a "fluid" moving through a patient's body. He noticed that in the passive state in which the patient was rendered, he could affect the direction or movement of this invisible fluid. He called this the "magnetic fluid" and posited its existence in every physical thing and that it had observable physical effects, especially healing. Mesmer developed a system of healing involving the movement of the magnetic fluid by a trained operator that resulted in patients entering a completely passive state, which Mesmer referred to as the "somnambulistic" state.[27] This was the precursor of modern hypnotism and the etymological origin for the term *mesmerized*.

In 1871 the Rosicrucian, Freemason, and English lord Edward Bulwer-Lytton anonymously published a novel about an extremely similar substance—an energy he called *vril* and described as an "all-permeating fluid."[28] In the 1930s, an identical form of energy was proposed by the Austrian physician and influential psychoanalyst Wilhelm Reich, which he referred to as *orgone*. Reich described the substance as a cosmic energy and not only theoretically posited it but also claimed to have observed it and demonstrated its existence.[29] Orgone was itself inspired in part by the philosopher Henri Bergson's *elan vital*, or "vital force." Henri was the brother of Mina Bergson, also known as

---

26. Franz Anton Mesmer, *Mesmerism: The Discovery of Animal Magnetism*, trans. V. R. Meyers (Boulder, CO: Soul Care Publishing, 2016), 28–30.

27. Mesmer, *Mesmerism*, 17.

28. Edward Bulwer-Lytton, *The Coming Race* (New York: Henry L. Hinton, 1873), 34, 54.

29. James DeMeo, *The Orgone Accumulator Handbook* (Ashland, OR: Natural Energy Works, 1989), 13.

Moina Mathers, the wife of occultist and ceremonial magician Samuel Liddell Mathers, who cofounded the Hermetic Order of the Golden Dawn, of which Moina was also an initiate. I mentioned earlier that Éliphas Lévi referred to the æther as azoth. Aside from his descriptions of the azoth as a universal magical agent and as a fluidic fire, Lévi also states, "[F]or the body it is quintessence, which is a combination of gold and light."[30]

The etymological origin of the word *azoth* comes from the Arabic *al-za'uq*, meaning "mercury," alluding to the universal mercury of the alchemists.[31] Azoth or æther, as we mentioned earlier in this book was elaborated by Éliphas Lévi as being "magnetized electricity."[32] In another description, by Manly Palmer Hall, we find azoth equated with the fiery waters of the rivers of Eden, the Hebrew *shamayim*, which literally means "fiery waters," with which creative Deity fashioned the cosmos.[33]

In fact, the entire universe is a vibratory dance of harmony, dissonance, and various kinds of physical manifestation of the different energetic-vibratory spectrum. Light, color, sound, and the phases of the elements—rapidity, volatility, fluidity, density—are all different manifestations in the greater cosmic ætheric field, within which the skilled practitioner—the magician—uses their knowledge and conscious intention to select, extract, amplify, attenuate, and direct various types of forces. These forces are all permeated by the quintessence, spirit, the universal mercury, azoth—the æther. Æther, therefore, while permeating all things, is also the energetic field from which they emerge as particular kinds of force. The nineteenth- and early twentieth–century Serbian-American engineer and inventor Nikola Tesla, known for his many contributions to the burgeoning field of early technological innovation, once wrote, "Long ago [humankind] recognized that all perceptible matter comes from a primary substance, of a tenuity beyond conception, filling all space, the Akasa or luminiferous ether, which is acted upon by the life-giving Prana or creative force, calling into existence, in never ending cycles, all things and phenomena."[34]

---

30. Éliphas Lévi, *Transcendental Magic: Its Doctrine and Ritual,* trans. Arthur Edward Waite (Chicago: De Laurence & Scott, 1910), 304.

31. *Merriam-Webster Dictionary*, s.v. "azoth," accessed April 15, 2024, https://www.merriam-webster.com/dictionary/azoth.

32. Lévi, *The Science of Hermes,* 10.

33. Manly P. Hall, *The Secret Teachings of All Ages: An Encyclopedic Outline of Masonic, Hermetic, Qabbalistic and Rosicrucian Symbolical Philosophy* (San Francisco: H. S. Crocker, 1928; electronic reproduction by J. B. Hare, Internet Sacred Texts Archive, 2001), 486.

34. John O'Neill, *Prodigal Genius: Biography of Nikola Tesla* (Long Island, NY: 1944; repr., Albuquerque, NM: Brotherhood of Life, 1994), 219.

SEEING THE ÆTHER

What can you expect ætheric energy or the spiritus animatus to look and feel like? We find it described as a fluid-like fire and as having the characteristics of light and magnetism. For the most part, these are helpful descriptors. You will find in the preliminary exercises to help you awaken the field of ætheric energy that there are different strata of æther relative to their proximity to the physical body. There is an inner layer, an area on average extended about two to five inches from the physical body, which can most readily be seen in the area of a person's shoulders and head. This layer appears to be luminescent, radiating an often white or light bluish glow. This white luminescence is diffused throughout the body.

Seeing the Sphere of Sensation

Oftentimes, when ætheric sight is at a significant level of development, the sphere of sensation appears as a radiant, wispy outline or double of the body, which can leave something akin to trails as the body moves from one position or location to another. This is true not only of human bodies but of all physical objects. The next outermost layer appears more like a haze of light, and the ætheric energy there takes on less of a fixed nature in that energy observed there can appear to move erratically, taking an almost cloudlike form varying in color and shape.

The outermost boundary of the sphere of sensation can be more difficult to perceive visually and, in most cases, is not entirely intact. That is, it does not enclose an individual the way many drawings depict it—rather, it can appear splotchy, broken, or completely missing. This may have to do with the increasing level of toxic intake by way of additives and other chemicals to our food, water, and air. The physical body (Qabalistically: *G'uph*) and the ætheric field (*Nephesch*) are aspects of one whole and are mutually interactive on an integral level.[35] This boundary is typically located about an arm's length in any direction from the individual's torso. The work of nineteenth-century British medical electrician Walter John Kilner is one of the best sources of information on the appearance of the "human atmosphere," his term for the aura or sphere of sensation.[36] Kilner's work was significant in pioneering methods of demonstrating the human energy field by inventing glass panels treated with colored dye solutions acting as a light filter through which different areas of the energetic field were visible. He categorized these into three distinct layers: the etheric double, the inner aura, and the outer aura.

---

35. Powell, *The Etheric Double*, 10.

36. Walter John Kilner, *The Human Atmosphere: or, The Aura Made Visible by the Aid of Chemical Screens* (New York: Rebman Company, 1911), 5.

These layers of the sphere of sensation can be palpated by the ætheric magic practitioner, as a preliminary diagnostic examination of their microcosmic ætheric field.

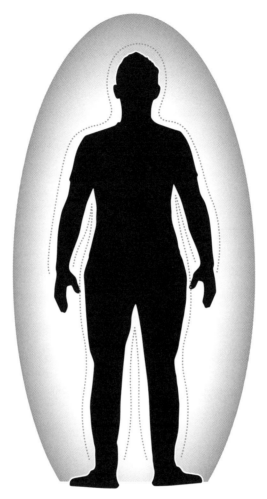

Kilner Screen Image

The Water Analogy

In the physical body, ætheric energy has consistently been conceived of as having a distinctly fluidlike movement. For instance, in Chinese medicine, in the study and nomenclature of the meridians of energy that run through the human body, otherwise known as channels and points, qi is consistently compared to bodies of water. For example, the width and depth of a channel of qi in the body corresponds to a sea, river, spring, stream, and so on. The acupuncture points are little areas where these waterways form whirlpools. They are essentially hundreds of small points of energy all over the human body, which can be utilized like circuitry of the ætheric-energetic system. These points have names like "bubbling spring," "sea of qi," and "elbow marsh." This is helpful not only as a descriptor of the quality of movement and perception of qi/ætheric energy but also in training the mind to think of the entirety of the human organism as a landscape, which is in constant interaction with itself. The health of this energetic system can be ascertained and labeled with certain diagnostic terms like *stagnation* (think of a stagnating pond) or *rebellion* (flowing counter to its natural direction).

An important thing to remember here is that this energy is impressionable not only to exterior environs and toxins, but also to the interior landscape of our minds and emotional states. Things such as depression can create stagnation of the energy, a heavy, dense, and sinking feeling not only in our hearts and minds but in our energy, which can in turn create a feedback loop, otherwise known as a vicious cycle. Thankfully, there are ways to kickstart our recovery, by way of moving the energy again. As the saying goes in Chinese medicine and related communities, "Where the mind goes, the qi flows."

The Dantian Centers

In the energy system of Chinese medicine, there are power centers called *dantian*, which correspond to certain areas of human anatomy. The dantian are areas within the trunk of the body where energy is thought to accumulate (often referred to as an elixir) and act as a reservoir corresponding to the specific aspects of individual activity, such as conscious awareness, love, and manifestation. In the ætheric magic system, we will refer to these as *alchemical centers*. Within the dantian or alchemical centers is a higher concentration of ætheric energy, which we can think of as storage batteries of the psyche-ætheric organism. Its location is related to how this energy is used and what functions it assists. Ultimately, the energies of these three centers must be in a harmonious alignment. In the case of an energetic deficiency, which is an etiology in Chinese medicine, these centers can be consciously used to accumulate and store ætheric energy. This is a foundational practice in the art of qigong.

The Chakra System

In the Vedic system of India, from which the various forms of yoga derive, ætheric energy is conceived as forming whirlpools, similar to the acupoints of Chinese medicine. These are called *chakras* in the Vedic system, meaning "wheels." Similarly to the dantian of the Chinese energetic model, the chakras most familiar to Westerners run along the centerline of the body and correspond to particular kinds of human activity such as instinct, loving kindness, communication, and the imaginal faculty. They run parallel and anterior to the human spine and correspond to the central column of energy (called *shushumna* in kriya yoga) through which kundalini is raised from the sacrum to the crown of the head. The chakra system is as follows:

Muladhara, **the Root Chakra:** Located at the base of the spine; corresponding to the physical body and survival instincts

Svadisthana, **the Sacral Chakra:** Located at the lower abdomen; corresponding to the generative instinct and sexuality

Manipura, **the Solar Plexus Chakra:** Located between the navel and diaphragm; corresponding to personal power and assertiveness

Anahata, **the Heart Chakra:** Located at the center of the chest; corresponding to expansive love

Vishudda, **the Throat Chakra:** Located at the base of the throat; corresponding to communication

Ajna, **the Third Eye Chakra:** Located at the center of the brow about one inch directly above the glabella or space between the eyebrows; corresponded to intuition, dreams, and visions

Sahasrara, **the Crown Chakra:** Located at the crown of the head; corresponding to intelligence and connection with the Divine

Though we will not necessarily be working with the Vedic system of chakras, there are obvious areas of overlap, and the associations of the chakra system will help augment our understanding of the overall mapping and correspondences of the individual energy system.

SOMATIC SENSATIONS

The stimulation or awakening of ætheric energy can be felt at various points on the body, such as at the crown, the point of the third eye (above and between the eyebrows), and in the center of the palms of the hands, for instance. The accompanying sensation can be described as white hot, a swirling sensation, or as if someone were gently blowing on a particular area. Ætheric energy as sensed by the hands can feel like static electricity, having a distinctly electrical and magnetic quality. Oftentimes in energy work a limb or limbs may feel as if they are being pulled in a particular direction and pulled or pushed apart by an unseen force, like a magnet. In the central column or Middle Pillar, it can also feel like a cool heat and, if moved very quickly, can sometimes be overwhelming.

I recommend that you keep a separate journal or space in your current magical one to record your own sensations of ætheric energy as you begin to stimulate and link your conscious mind with it. Ætheric energy can be seen up close as it moves through the hands. It appears almost as a static radiance, similar to steam rising off of a hot road and television static. Different hues can be indicative of different qualities of the energy. I will discuss this in more detail in later chapters on beginning practice.

CONCLUSION

Ætheric energy has been further studied under many different names by several prominent innovators throughout the West. Some of these innovators profoundly affected Western culture with their discoveries concerning the æther. I have shown you how the careful examination of older literature can be undertaken to gain greater insight to the practice of magic and healing. While different systems have developed between the East and the West, they are ultimately reconcilable and indeed important in achieving a holistic understanding of the greater ætheric picture.

CHAPTER 4

MAPPING THE MICROCOSM

In the ætheric magic system, I will utilize a mapping system known as the Qabalistic Tree of Life as our ground plan for cultivating and moving ætheric energy around the anatomical body and broader ætheric field or sphere of sensation. This will necessitate some knowledge of the diagrammatic image of the Tree of Life, which comprises the ten *sephiroth*, or spheres, and twenty-two *netivoth*, or paths. I mentioned earlier the doctrine of the macrocosm and microcosm; the Tree of Life is a glyph by which we may conceptualize the constituent forces that compose material existence on both macrocosmic and microcosmic scales, as well as their relationships to one another. In short, it is a conceptual model of all that is—the blueprint of existence within both the individual and the greater cosmos.

QABALAH AND THE TREE OF LIFE

The modern system of Qabalah is a product of nineteenth- and twentieth-century occultists appropriating and evolving earlier forms of the system that they inherited in the form of texts, such as *The Kabbalah Unveiled* by the seventeenth-century German Hebraist and scholar Christian Knorr von Rosenroth. This work was famously translated out of its original Latin by the nineteenth-century occultist and cofounder of the Hermetic Order of the Golden Dawn, Samuel Liddell Mathers. In this iteration of Qabalah, which is spelled with a *Q* as a convention to designate it as a later development of distinct earlier traditions, earlier methods of mystical exegesis typically applied to Hebrew scriptural texts were applied to a broader scope of study, such as the tarot, astrology, and various other arts falling within the *fin-de-siècle* occult milieu.

The diagram of the Tree of Life was the conceptual basis for much of the system of correspondences developed by occult initiates working within this system in the nineteenth and twentieth centuries and is still a foundational component of modern forms of magic. Diagrammatically, the Tree of Life is composed of lines and circles—the netivoth and sephiroth, or paths and spheres. The Tree of Life also corresponds to human anatomy and types of force or energy within the ætheric field, exemplified in the sephiroth.

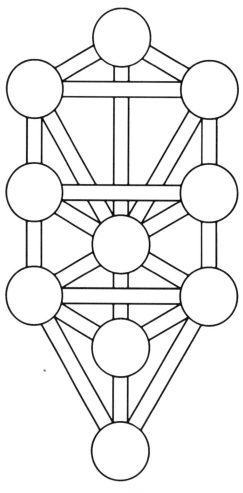

Tree of Life

The Spheres

The tree is conceived as the downward emanation of the forces of creation out of three veils of negative existence—incomprehensible and diffuse eternity—beginning with the sephirah *Kether* ("crown"), successively emanating like a lightning bolt down to *Malkuth* ("kingdom"). The sephiroth and their correspondences are as follows:

Kether, "Crown"

The first sephirah in order of succession, Kether is referred to as the first cause, unity consciousness. It represents the absolute unity that precedes and generates all creation. This sephirah is referred to as the first movements of the material universe, stirring to activity and coming into creation. Kether corresponds anatomically to the crown of the head and just above it.

Chokmah, "Wisdom"

The second emanation, corresponding to the archetype of force—a projection or moving outward. Chokmah also corresponds to the sphere of the fixed stars of medieval and Renaissance cosmology and the zodiacal wheel. It anatomically corresponds to the left side of the face and head.

Binah, "Understanding"

Third in order of emanation, completing what is referred to as the *supernal triad*. Binah corresponds to the archetype of form—a condensation—and corresponds to the planetary sphere of Saturn, the outermost planet in the classical model of the solar system. Binah anatomically corresponds to the right side of the face and head.

Da'ath, "Knowledge"

Da'ath is not a proper sephirah but has traditionally been an essential point of designation on the tree. Da'ath acts as a focal point for the supernals to emanate downward into creation and is also often referred to as an abyss.

Chesed, "Mercy"

Fourth in order of emanation and separated from the supernal triad Da'ath, this sephirah corresponds to the principle or archetype of three-dimensional stability, the beginning of creation, which is expansion. While the geometric figures of the point, line, and triangle correspond to the supernals of Kether, Chokmah, and Binah respectively, the cube—a geometrical figure possessing height, width, and depth—corresponds to Chesed. As the essence of stable expansion, rather than the diffuse projection of Chokmah, Chesed aptly corresponds to the planetary sphere of Jupiter. Anatomically, this sephirah corresponds to the left shoulder and arm.

Geburah, "Severity"

The fifth in order of succession, Geburah represents the principle of severity. Rather than simply viewing this sephirah as something malicious, we should conceive of it as the aspect of creation that prevents instability by overgrowth. In other words, it is a counterbalance to the expansion of Chesed in the same way naturally occurring forest fires serve to organically reset the biome of an area overpopulated by trees and other flora. This sephirah is alternately referred to as justice and corresponds to the planetary sphere of Mars. Geburah corresponds anatomically to the right shoulder and arm.

Tiphareth, "Beauty"

The sixth and central sephirah, Tiphareth corresponds to the mediating principle, which is the representative of unity amid multiplicity. As Kether ("crown") expresses the unity preceding creation, Tiphareth represents unity in the midst of creation. It can be seen as the center of gravity, occupying the space at the center of the tree. As such, it aptly corresponds to the central body of our solar system—the sun. It corresponds anatomically to the center of the chest.

Netzach, "Victory"

Seventh in order of succession, Netzach represents passion, as the fire of Geburah passes through the beauty and love of Tiphareth. Situated directly beneath Chesed on the Pillar of Mercy, Neztach is the passion that ignites creativity and the spirit to fight in defense of those we love. It corresponds to the planetary sphere of Venus and anatomically to the left hip.

Hod, "Glory"

Eighth in order of succession, Hod represents the intellective faculties of the mind and the part of the psyche that looks outward, analyzing what it sees with discursive reasoning. As representative of intellectual pursuits, the swiftness of the mind, and intelligent communication, Hod corresponds to the planetary sphere of Mercury and anatomically to the right hip.

Yesod, "Foundation"

Ninth in order of succession, Yesod is the lowermost before Malkuth (the final sephirah in succession) and represents the subconscious, wherein the content of dreams and visions burgeons forth and manifests. It is through Yesod that all the aforementioned sephirah must pass and be directed into physical manifestation in Malkuth, and therefore, Yesod can be seen as a kind of blueprint of physical reality. It corresponds to the sphere of the moon and the pelvic and genital region of the human anatomy.

Malkuth, "Kingdom"

The tenth and final sephirah on the Tree of Life, Malkuth represents the ground of physical manifestation of all the preceding sephiroth. It is referred to in Qabalistic literature as the gateway into incarnation and a container in which all the essences of the tree pour, congeal, and manifest as individual physical existences. It is referred to as the quaternary of the elements—fire, air, water, and earth—and anatomically corresponds to the feet and the ground immediately below the feet.

RELATIONSHIPS OF THE SEPHIROTH

As I briefly mentioned earlier, the sephirothic spheres are conceptualized as representing particular essences or forces. The sephiroth are conceived as individualized expressions of potentials within the mind of the Divine. The uppermost triad of sephiroth comprises Kether, Chokmah, and Binah, referred to jointly as the supernal triad, which are typically colored white, gray, and black, respectively. Kether ("crown") represents the monad of divinity, first burgeoning forth from the unmanifest. Chokmah ("wisdom") corresponds to the principle of force—similar to the celestial niter—or the active principle. Binah ("understanding") corresponds to the principle of form—similar to our celestial salt—or the receptive principle. Force without form has no ground and is consequently dissipated and wasted. Form without force is un-enlivened, inanimate, and utterly inert.

You might view the remaining seven sephiroth below Da'ath similarly to the seven colors of the rainbow, which separate out of a beam of pure white light when passing through a prism. Therefore, we could look at Da'ath as the prism point on the Tree of Life, though again it is not a proper sephirah. These are the psycho-æetheric constituents of the individual, which are collectively termed the *ruach*, or breath/spirit of the microcosm. This part of the tree is composed of two inverted triangles, in contradistinction to the upright triangle of the supernals. On this side of Da'ath—the abyss—this intimates a reflective characteristic to the lower part of the tree. Successively, we have the sephirah Chesed ("mercy"), corresponding to the color blue, the essence of growth and expansion, followed by Geburah ("severity"), corresponding to the color red and the essence of limitation, restriction, or restraint. The equilibrating sephirah poised below and between the two is Tiphareth ("beauty"), corresponding to the color yellow and the harmony that is affected in the balancing of mercy and severity—the blending of expansion and limitation. These three sephiroth exhibit by their colors the three primary colors and are referred to as the ethical triangle of the Tree of Life.

The following triangle is composed of the sephirah Netzach ("victory"), corresponding to the color green and the passions and emotional nature in an individual. The sephirah Hod ("glory") corresponds to the color orange, and the sephirah Yesod ("foundation") corresponds to the color violet. This triangle (Netzach-Hod-Yesod) is referred to as the mental triangle. Appended to this triangle is the tenth and final sephirah on the Tree of Life—Malkuth ("kingdom"), corresponding to the four colors citrine, olive, russet, and black and to the physical substances composing the material body.

The Three Pillars

This arrangement of the Tree of Life gives us three pillars or columns of sephiroth, with three on the right, three on the left, and four (five when we include the unofficial sephirah Da'ath) along the central column. In the ætheric magic system, we will be working mostly with the sephiroth that are aligned along the central column, also known as the Middle Pillar. We work primarily with the Middle Pillar because this pillar corresponds to the central channel of energy and the spine, along which run the major energy centers of the Eastern and Western systems (chakras and sephiroth) as well as the three dantian. Also, the Middle Pillar is the most direct path in grounding spiritual energy and raising secret fire.

The Paths

The sephiroth of the Tree of Life are connected by the paths, which are themselves corresponded to various colors, other ideas, and symbolic correspondences and represent experiential dimensions of life. Rather than the concentrated, static nature of the essences corresponding to the sephiroth, the paths represent the meeting points and blending of essences between each sephirah they connect. They are also conduits of the directional flow of energy within the Tree. The paths each correspond to various astrological and elemental correspondences. These do not need to be memorized for the system of ætheric magic, but it is encouraged. For ease of reference, the traditional correspondences of the spheres and paths on the Tree of Life are listed in appendix B.

Some magical practitioners may find the strict use of these systems of correspondences somewhat tedious or restrictive. However, all magic deals in working with things that are largely intangible or to some degree abstract, and therefore, symbols become the vocabulary with which we may reliably call upon a force or forces with a degree of precision.

The letters of the Hebrew alphabet are also attributed to each of the twenty-two paths; however, for our work, only the three "Mother" letters will need to be memorized. These are *aleph* (א), *mem* (מ), and *shin* (ש), transliterated to the Latin letters *A*, *M*, and *S(h)*, respectively. These represent certain sounds as well as ideas. Mem, associated with the element of water, is considered silent since the lips are closed. However, when vibrated or intoned, it is hummed as an *Mmm* sound. Shin, corresponding to elemental fire, is sibilant and when vibrated generates a *Shh* sound. Aleph is the tongue of balance between the two and, corresponding to elemental air, makes an *Ahh* sound when vibrated or intoned. Being representative of the creative elements, water, air, and fire, these can be further corresponded to the alchemical Tria Prima of salt (water), mercury (air), and sulfur (fire). These three elements, inclusive of their correspondences to the Tria Prima, will be utilized in the ætheric magic system as power centers (dantian) along the Middle Pillar (centerline).

The Four Worlds

The planes and bodies also correspond to the Four Worlds of the Qabalah. The Qabalistic worlds include the following:

> **Atziluth:** The Spiritual/Archetypal World, corresponding to the spiritual plane
>
> **Briah:** The Creative World, corresponding to the mental plane
>
> **Yetzirah:** The Formative World, corresponding to the astral plane
>
> **Assiah:** The Physical World/World of Action, corresponding to the ætheric-physical plane

There is a Fifth World, which is little spoken of, that corresponds to the transcendent reality of the infinite.

BRINGING THE SYSTEMS TOGETHER

In esoteric Taoist energy theory and systems of Chinese medicine, there are three major energy centers located at points along the central axis of the body. These are called the three *dantian,* also referred to as the "three diamonds" in the Japanese system of energy work *reiki,* pioneered by Mikao Usui. These energy centers are considered to contain certain vital essences corresponding to consciousness, essence, and vital energy. To these, we ascribe our Tria Prima:

Salt corresponds to the lower dantian, at the lower abdominal cavity, corresponding to elemental water, the essence—a concentration of vital energy that is also linked to the astral "blueprint" of the individual and expressed by things such as genetics and associated with the sephiroth Malkuth and Yesod. The middle dantian at the center of the chest cavity, corresponding to mercury, elemental air, the vital lifeforce energy of an individual, is related to the sephirah Tiphareth. Finally, we have the upper dantian, located in the cranial cavity, which is accessible through the third eye, sometimes called by the Latin title *Uncia Coeli,* or UC, meaning "the little heaven" and corresponding to sulfur, elemental fire, and the consciousness, totality of psychic faculties, and presence of an individual. This center corresponds to the sephiroth Da'ath and Kether.

We will picture the outermost boundary of the sphere of sensation (aura) as a large hermetically sealed vessel when performing our work, a container within which we circulate, purify, and refine the various elixirs within our ætheric-psyche-spiritual architecture. With this model, we can view the body and greater ætheric field inclusive of the sphere of sensation as an alchemical vehicle—the Salt Center acting as a crucible or cauldron, the Sulfur Center acting as an ambix or distillation head, and the Mercury Center acting as a kind of alembic, participating in a two-way interaction either with the lower Salt Center or upper Sulfur Center, a mediator for the movement of ætheric energy.

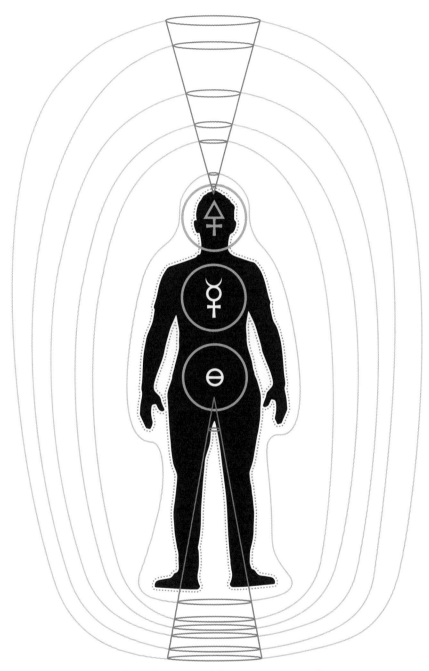

Full Body Image of the Hermetic Vessel

LOCATIONS OF SIGNIFICANCE

There are two locations of significance that are situated at either extreme of the body—the sole of both feet and the crown of the head. At each of these points is a *dini,* the Greek term for "whirlpool" or "vortex" (referred to in other systems as "acupoints" or "chakras") between the size of a dime and a quarter, which we will "activate" through various visualizations during our work in the ætheric magic system. At the crown and midline of the head, in line with the apex of the ears, we will call this the Spirit Crown Point. The dines (*DEE-neez,* plural of dini) located near the balls of the feet we will refer to as the Earth Root Points.

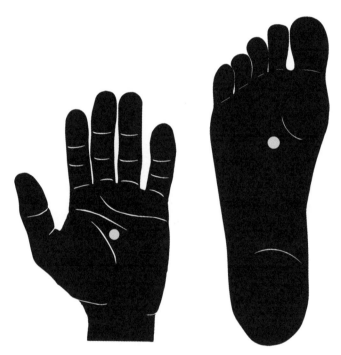

Hand Point and Foot Point

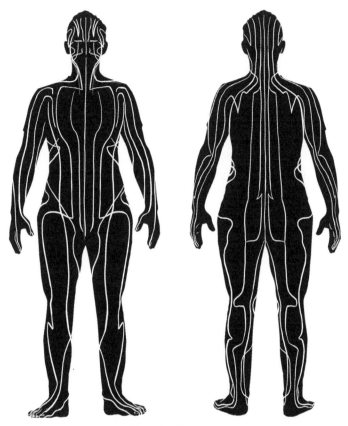

Full Body Flow Diagram

There are important energetic considerations in the hands and face as well. The hands are one of the most readily accessible tools in the tactile perception of ætheric energy. The left and right hands can be considered in relation to the principals of celestial salt and celestial niter, respectively. That is, at the center of each palm is a dini, which we will refer to as the Projection and Reception Points, which correspond to the reception and projection of ætheric energy. Both points can be used to project or receive; however, typically, the left hand is thought of as the receptive, and the right hand is considered projective.

There have been contradictory accounts concerning the idea of dominant versus non-dominant hand rather than left versus right hand in the projection of ætheric energy. Some practitioners aver that the projection hand is always the right hand, while others claim that the dominant hand is always the hand which should be used to project. This should be resolved by individual practitioner experimentation. When you have reached the sections on energy projection in this book, pay special attention to the sensation of energy moving through the hands and decide for yourself what feels right.

For now, I'll designate these as passive and active by the following signs: – and +. Further, each finger has an elemental attribution: the thumb to spirit/quintessence, the index finger to water, middle finger to earth, ring finger to fire, and little finger to air. The orifices of the face correspond to specific planetary influences, which have associated elemental correspondences: the right eye corresponds to the sun; the left eye to the moon. The right nostril corresponds to Mars; the left to Venus. The right ear corresponds to Saturn and the left to Jupiter, while the mouth corresponds to Mercury. These are general correspondences that will not figure very heavily in our work, but I have included them in order to be thorough.

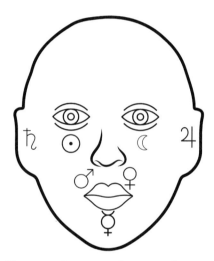

Planetary Correspondences in the Face

ENERGY MOVEMENT

Last, I'll share the particular pathways of the flow of ætheric energy, of which there are several. These constructs will aid our movement of ætheric energy through the body and the greater ætheric vehicle of the sphere of sensation. Beginning from the center-most position and moving outward, we have the Middle Pillar or center pathway, which corresponds to the spinal column and also extends into and passes through the major cavities of the torso—abdomen, chest, etc.—extending down to the feet. Through this central channel, we will pull in and move ætheric energy using breath work, vibration (mantra), and focused visualizations in both upward and downward directions through the various sephiroth of the Middle Pillar and our three alchemical centers.

The next pathway is called the Microcosmic Pathway. This pathway runs along the outermost layer of the body, in a kind of circuit. It begins in the perineum and runs vertically up the back of the body, to the top of the head, and from there descends again in a vertical line back down the front of the body, back to the perineum. This ætheric pathway generally runs in this direction of flow in a healthy individual—up the back and down the front. There is also the horizontal pathway, which essentially encircles the lower abdomen by way of the hips. Finally, there is the movement of ætheric energy around the sphere of sensation in various directions.

CONCLUSION

Understanding the microcosm of the self is an important aspect of magic. The elements, planets, stars, and universal forces reside within the magician. To seize these forces, you must be able to find them within yourself. The models we utilize—the Tria Prima, the sphere of sensation, and the Tree of Life—are effective systems that will allow you to come to understand not only these forces within you but also the ways in which they interact with each other. These systems also allow your mind access to pathways of consciousness and the movement of ætheric energy to and through these various forces and centers of force—they are the scaffolding with which the ætheric magician is built.

CHAPTER 5
THE ELEMENTAL SELF

Before diving into practice, I should mention a few things of which it is important to remain aware as you progress through this work. The psyche-ætheric self, which is the aspect of the individual represented by the sephiroth Malkuth through Netzach, can be viewed as elemental in nature. In other words, aspects of our interior psyche are a blended whole comprising various aspects that have their own individuated spheres of expression but also work in relationship and interaction with each other. These elements and aspects of the self are intimately linked with our individual ætheric field and, in some instances, with the ætheric fields of others. When we begin to stimulate or "awaken" our ætheric energy to movement with our conscious minds, we essentially begin breaking what can be, for some, long-established patterns.

EFFECTS OF ÆTHERIC ALCHEMY

Continuing with the water analogy I mentioned in chapter 3, you might think of the flow of ætheric energy in a similar way to water training grooves into the earth, establishing its routes of flow and accumulation. When these patterns are not intentional but rather a product of automatic reactions, they can cause or contribute to negative mental and behavioral patterns like addiction and emotional imbalance, and over time, these things can cause physical illness to manifest. What's more, phenomena such as psychological complexes—things that trigger an automatic mental and behavioral response trajectory—bind up ætheric energy into little loops, which keeps the energy from flowing freely and diminishes our access to available energy that would otherwise increase our effectiveness and power in magical operations.

This is one of several reasons for the elemental trajectory of spiritual alchemy, which we find prerequisite to large-scale magical operation in the outer Order rituals of the Golden Dawn and derivative organizations. When the alchemists of old spoke of the "Elements of the Wise" or "Our" fire, water, air, or earth, they were not speaking of the actual material substances of each as such. In spiritual and inner alchemy, when we say the "elements," we mean the super-essential qualities that influence states of matter in various combinations and permutations, the patterns and interactions influencing the way all material things move and change.

The elemental self will undergo a "deep clean," so to speak, in this reorganization of ætheric energy throughout the sphere of sensation and can consequently affect our lives in often unexpected ways. Long-held structures and beliefs may find themselves subject to change as a consequence of this reorganization. This can present us with an opportunity for greater healing and a liminal space within which to create a new vision of our futures. Oftentimes these changes may not seem "spiritual" but rather mundane.

In any case, the areas in which we experience change are most likely associated with strengths, weaknesses, and blind spots to both that we previously had. Some may develop new skills and sharper acuity of consciousness following the release of previously bound-up ætheric energy. Issues of finances, physical health, and well-being, for instance, will correspond to elemental earth in our spheres of sensation; challenges of passion, anger, and courage will correspond to elemental fire. Rather than merely moving this energy so that it releases itself for availability from a bound state, you will utilize and develop techniques in chapters 6 through 9 for channeling it toward healing, internal alchemy, and magic—a harmony of the elements.

It should be clarified that ætheric energy is inherently psycho-sexual in nature. We should attempt to conceive of sexuality on a broader, macrocosmic level for a moment. Human sexual reproduction is a microcosmic manifestation of the greater essence of sexuality, which is the creative impulse. This fiery water permeates everything in the entire cosmos—what is the cosmos but a constant dance of destruction and creation? Ætheric energy is the magical agent because it is a formative, creative substance. This said, the densest accumulation of it is in the alchemical cauldron—the Salt Center corresponding to the lower dantian and the sephirothic axis of Malkuth-Yesod. The movement and accumulation of energy will stimulate a cascade of impulses, the lowest manifestation of which is the individual sexual drive of the practitioner. This, like most things, is not bad in and of itself, but it is certainly something to be aware of, particularly if an uptick in sex drive is something unwanted by an individual practitioner or if the practitioner has issues in this area with self-control. The elemental/alchemical nature of the ætheric magic system will help mitigate disproportionate behavioral responses due to accumulation of ætheric energy.

ÆTHER AND THE ELEMENTS OF THE WISE

While ætheric energy itself is most often latent in most individuals and generally typified as having more of a quintessential nature, it contains specific qualities that correspond to the quaternary of the elements (i.e., fire, air, water, and earth). Each element corresponds to a type of frequency or energetic quality that is generated in the ætheric field—mostly unconsciously—by the individual. Anger may manifest more of a fiery quality within the ætheric field; melancholy may manifest more of a watery quality.

These elemental energies are contained within the energy of the ætheric field and activate in accordance with the mental-emotional states of the individual. The ætheric magic practitioner is able to generate these elemental qualities in their sphere of sensation at will for the purposes of mood specificity and energy requirements. Say you were feeling lethargic—earth—and wanted to generate a more energetic quality—fire. Or if you were feeling the need to become more grounded and in your own body, you might generate an earthy quality in your sphere of sensation. This is done by visualization and generating mental states that correspond to each elemental aspect of the self.

Eastern Systems

To bring some clarity to the subject of elemental fluctuations of the æther, let's look at some well-established Eastern systems of the elements. The system of the *tattvas* is an elemental system of ætheric tides or cycles of elemental permutation of the macrocosmic æthers of the planet Earth. This system was developed by the Tamil Siddhas of ancient India, a shamanic group of healers in the esoteric Vedic tradition. Based on a five-element model, the tattvas are as follows:

Tejas (Fire): Represented by a red triangle

Prithivi (Earth): Represented by a yellow square

Apas (Water): Represented by a silver crescent

Vayu (Air): Represented by a blue circle

Akasa (Spirit): Represented by a purple egg

TEJAS	PRITHIVI	APAS	VAYU	AKASA
FIRE	EARTH	WATER	AIR	SPIRIT
Red	Yellow	Silver	Blue	Purple

Tattva Diagram

The first of these elements, *akasa*, or spirit, is the substantive ground within which all the other elements have their existence. The quaternary elements burgeon forth from akasa and permeate with each other in constant mixture, with one or another predominating the mixture in certain material manifestations and time periods. The important idea here is that they are inextricably mixed with one another and are subject to flux—one dominates in a specific instance, such as, say, the earth element of *prithivi* in a tree, yet is tied to all the others. The roots and trunk have a basis in earth, yet the tree interacts with the other elements in photosynthesis—the absorption of sunlight (fire), water, and oxygen (air) as food.

In Taoist elemental theory, the same relationship between the elements is present in certain cycles corresponding to elemental change, generation, and counteroperation in the diagram of the elemental pentagram called the *wu xing*, or "five phases."

Though the Taoist system of elements is slightly different from the traditional Western and Vedic, the five phases demonstrate the same permutative cycle of the elements as we have seen in the tattva system and which the ætheric magic practitioner may utilize when conceptualizing the æther in general. These cycles apply to both macrocosmic cycles (cosmic and terrestrial phenomena) and microcosmic cycles (mental, emotional, and bodily phenomena) as exemplified by the conceptual model of macrocosm and microcosm that I developed in chapters 2 and 4. I'll now go through the elements as they are conceived in the ætheric magic system.

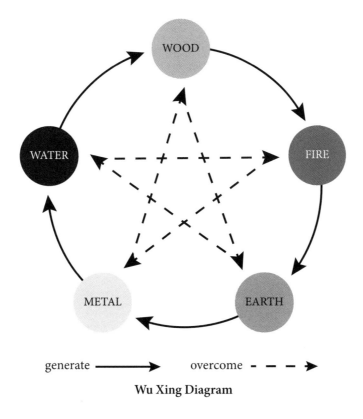

generate ——————→   overcome - - - →

Wu Xing Diagram

This concept of the elements as permutative and participatory with one another is important in ætheric magic because the ætheric magic practitioner will use specific visualizations, postures, and times to cycle through the ætheric elements in their own sphere of sensation in order to bring one to the fore for a work of healing or elemental talismanic consecration, for instance. You can also tie these to the planetary bodies, and they can be used in tandem with planetary hours based on elemental associations attributed to the planetary bodies. Here is a list of planetary elemental correspondences for your reference:

Saturn: Earth
Mars: Fire
Jupiter: Air

Sun: Fire (also has an affinity with spirit)

Venus: Fire (sometimes also water and earth)

Mercury: Air (also has an affinity with water)

Moon: Water

I will go over this in more detail in the practical chapters of this book.

SPIRIT

Spirit is synonymous with the quintessence and ætheric energy in its most general and unconditioned state. The practitioner of ætheric magic always begins by cultivating this quality of spirit in their personal ætheric field by achieving a state of relaxed concentration that is devoid of any strong emotional or mental state. This allows the practitioner to more easily, effectively, and intentionally cultivate a specific quality of the æther associated with a particular element within their sphere of sensation. Some general associations and correspondences of elemental spirit are as follows:

- Æther
- Gold
- Diamond
- The color white
- The planetary sphere of the Sun
- Solar deities
- Alchemical quintessence

FIRE

Typically, fire is associated with heat and dryness. As it is understood that heat energy is physically related to the expansion and rapid motion of molecules, fire represents the active principle of pure motion and expansion. It is active-active (+ , +) on the spectrum of permutation between the polarities. The ætheric magic practitioner would use elemental fire to cultivate energy in themselves. They might also use fire as the elemental impetus for the cultivation of characteristics of courage and assertiveness.

Fire can be focused and channeled through the sphere of sensation by association with and visualization of its known correspondences. Some correspondences of the element of fire are as follows:

- Heat and dryness
- Rapidity
- Motion
- Friction
- Ruby
- Tobacco
- The color red
- Anger/hot-temperedness
- The planetary sphere of Mars

AIR

Elemental air has attributes correspondent to movement as well, but it also has a component of moisture. As water vaporizes, it rises into the air, condenses, and creates clouds that send down rain upon the earth. The qualities of swiftness, travel, and exchange are also primary attributes of elemental air. This is exemplified in the winds, which can carry sounds and voices across distances as well as pollen to germinate across distances.

The ætheric magic practitioner would activate elemental air in their sphere of sensation for purposes of increased communication (being heard), intellectual swiftness and agility, and the consecration of a talisman or other magical implement to elemental air or the planetary spheres of Jupiter or Mercury, with which it has an elemental association. Air also has an affinity with æther in that they share similar attributes in that air participates in fluidity—at least much more so than fire (observe the way it moves)—and therefore it shares in the fluidlike nature of the movement of ætheric energy. Air is also thought to carry the æther in primeval elemental modalities of healing and magic like the Vedic tattva system and Taoist qi theory, as the sun's rays and moon's light appear to travel through with air. This is why the words for æther and breath, vapor, or air are the same in many of those systems (prana, qi, pneuma, ruach, etc.) and each involves working with the breath of the practitioner in order to cultivate and move energy. Some correspondences of air are as follows:

- Heat and moisture
- Swiftness
- Communication

- Travel
- Exchange
- Lapis lazuli
- Aromatic herbs
- The color yellow
- The planetary spheres of Jupiter and Mercury

WATER

Coldness and moisture are the characteristic qualities of elemental water, and it is associated with fluidity and shape-shifting (water takes the shape of the vessel which holds it). Purification is a primary attribute of water, in addition to life-giving properties. Think of how life on Earth grows out of water and how a developing infant grows in the amniotic fluid of the womb. Water also has a reflective quality that alludes to dreams, visions, and the astral plane. The ætheric magic practitioner can bring the element of water to the fore in their sphere of sensation for rites of purification, dream and vision work, and any working that corresponds to the sphere of the moon, which has an elemental affinity to water by way of its effect on Earth's tides and other bodies of water. The moon is also the receptive counterpart to the activity of the sun—it receives and reflects the rays of the sun's light, radiating them in the absence of the solar orb to their proverbial child, Earth. The planetary sphere of Venus also shares in this watery affinity in her iteration as the Greek goddess Aphrodite, whose name means "foam-born" and who has a strong correspondence to feminine sexuality.[37]

I should note that ætheric energy is indisputably affected by the moon. We find this in everything from humans and animals to the watery tides and growth of plants. In short, during the waxing and full lunar periods, ætheric energy is built up in the atmosphere and environment and, consequently, in the microcosmic sphere of sensation of the practitioner. During the waning and dark periods, ætheric energy becomes less available. This may have a direct correlation with things having to do with a grounding or earthy discharge of ætheric energy, such as relapse in addiction and stronger sexual impulses as the moon waxes full, over the course of the 29.5-day period of the lunar cycle. This also suggests a praxis of active, practical ætheric energy work and magic

---

37. "Aphrodite," Oxford Reference, accessed April 15, 2024, https://www.oxfordreference.com
/display/10.1093/oi/authority.20110803095418734.

during the waxing and full periods and more meditative, accumulative, inner work during the later waning and dark periods. This likely says something about the fluidlike nature of ætheric energy and the correspondence of the moon to the element of water.

Some correspondences of elemental water are as follows:

- Cold and moisture
- Fluidity
- Receptivity
- Reflectiveness
- Moonstone
- Plants that grow in marshes or near other bodies of water
- The color blue
- The planetary spheres of Venus and the Moon

EARTH

Elemental earth's qualities are coldness and dryness, as well as stability and growth. Earth is also associated with darkness, physicality, and limitation, as all forms manifested physically must have boundaries delineating their individuality, and seeds must be planted in the dark soil in order to grow to fruition. This element corresponds to the physical body of the practitioner, of which the ætheric body is a rarefied aspect. The planetary spheres of Earth and Saturn also correspond to elemental earth and are themselves associated with all the aforementioned qualities.

The ætheric magic practitioner brings elemental earth to the fore in their ætheric field for stability and growth in a particular area—usually their material lives. Saturnian expressions of this energy may be used to invoke discipline and limitations that ultimately serve to your benefit. This energy can also be applied to banishing and bindings in magical works of conjuration as well as attracting wealth if you are inclined to practice money magic.

Some correspondences of elemental earth are as follows:

- Density
- Growth and limitation
- Darkness
- Tiger's-eye

- Roots of plants, tubers
- Material wealth
- The colors green and black
- The planetary spheres of Earth and Saturn

CONCLUSION

The exploration of the microcosmic elements within yourself provides a strong foundation for the alchemical transmutation that ætheric magic catalyzes. The same exploration will also deepen your understanding of the qualities and permutations that manifest throughout the physical world in the all-pervading æther. The permutation of the elements manifesting in all things is a key to the art of magic, and becoming familiar with their flow and qualities will allow you to bring them forth and embody them in your sphere of sensation in your practical work within the ætheric magic system.

CHAPTER 6
AWAKENING THE ÆTHER

In this chapter, I'll focus primarily on two phases of the work over a series of several exercises geared toward the marriage of Sol and Luna, or the linking of the conscious mind to the ætheric field, bringing our ætheric energy under conscious command. The analogy of the marriage of Sol and Luna (sun and moon) was thought of in alchemy as the phase of completion in the Great Work. The phases of this work will be (1) perception of ætheric energy—seeing and feeling—and (2) the flow of ætheric energy—breathing and movement.

These elementary exercises should be persisted in until proficiency is achieved, and they are excellent refreshers for experienced practitioners. The practices can be added to and expanded as you develop your ætheric sight by experimenting with seeing the multiple distinct layers of the entire sphere of sensation or by noticing any changes in the color, shape, and other qualities of the energy depending on the mood, current activities, and any other internal or external factors that may be affecting the individual you are viewing. Again, you will gradually find that ætheric sight is more readily accessible or has fused with your active vision over time.

In my own experience, as time went on and my ætheric sight further developed, I began to practice in complete darkness. This became extremely helpful, as many of the variations of ætheric energy more difficult to see are sometimes easier to perceive in a completely darkened room, at least for some practitioners.

I emphatically recommend that you keep a record (journal) of all your experiences, whether they be sensations, thoughts, emotions, images, or anything else that arises just before, during, or after the performance of these exercises.

A NOTE ON SEALING THE CIRCUIT

Several of the following exercises will employ a technique referred to as *sealing the circuit*, or closing out. Sealing the circuit involves slow, controlled, and deliberate movements beginning with your arms hanging at your sides and then bringing them up over the top of your head in a circular motion, forming an arch there with your hands. From this point, bring your hands straight down in front of you along the centerline, also called the Middle Pillar. Your hands should be horizontal with palms downward. Bring them straight down until the point of your pelvis, or the Yesod Center. When you reach this area, bring the arms back up once more in the same deliberate, slow circular motion above your head. Repeat this a total of three times.

Closing Out 1

Closing Out 2

Closing Out 3

Closing Out 4

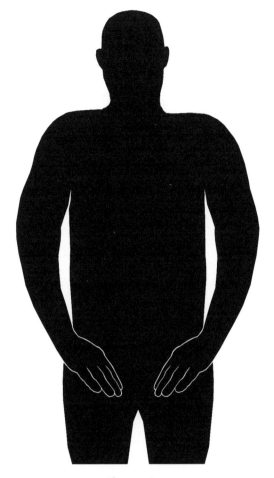

Closing Out 5

PHASE 1: SEEING

The first thing to be said about perceiving ætheric energy by way of sight is that when beginning, it will require us to retrain the way we see. The *type* of sight used to see ætheric energy is slightly different from the type of sight we use to see denser material objects. Usually, our eyes notice something—say, a bright red apple on a countertop—and then immediately, almost involuntarily, focus on that object. We acknowledge the qualities that designate it as an apple, and we move on to the next series of concrete objects. This is a very active type of sight.

However, the sight we use to see ætheric energy is more peripheral and passive. I compare this difference to the analogy of grasping water. If you reach out, attempting to grab water the same way you would grasp an apple, you will likely create nothing but a splashy mess. However, when you *relax* our hands, form a receptive cup shape with them, and gently receive the water, you will succeed. The same applies to your ætheric vision—you must begin with a relaxed gaze, not focusing on any particular object, almost staring, yet not allowing your awareness to wander off from the thing you are viewing. The tendency will be, once the various layers of energy become slightly perceptible, to immediately focus your eyes on it. This, however, will only serve to take you out of ætheric sight, and into active sight. So you must remain aware of the ætheric energy as it presents itself to you, while not focusing on and looking directly at it. Over time, these two types of vision will become fused. In fact, you may even need to practice techniques to balance them, so that your ætheric sight doesn't overwhelm your active sight while performing daily tasks.

Following are a series of elementary exercises to get you started. These exercises should be performed once a day, five to seven days a week, for one to two weeks, or longer depending on results.

EXERCISE: SKY GAZING

One of the best exercises to begin training our ætheric sight is to sky gaze. This technique allows you to develop and strengthen ætheric sight by introducing you to the type of sight needed to view the æther, as well as what this species of energy looks like. You will become acquainted with observing ætheric energy in the sphere of sensation. In some fortunate cases, it also has the effect of activating tactile perception of ætheric energy; sometimes activating one mode of perception simultaneously activates others.

The timing technique for this exercise is fairly simple—you will need mostly clear skies and a location in which you won't be distracted. On a clear day, find a spot outside where you can sit comfortably for about twenty minutes to a half hour. Remember, the key is to remain relaxed.

If you can't get outside due to weather or accessibility, this exercise can be continued indoors with a piece of blank, single-color paper or a completely bare wall or ceiling of a preferably light color.

Directions

1. Begin with a few deep belly breaths with long, slow exhalation. As you exhale, imagine your body, starting with your face, neck, and shoulders, completely relaxing. Feel your mental, emotional, and bodily tension and pain completely melt away. Do this as many times as needed to achieve a relaxed but alert state of mind and body.

2. Once this is achieved, look upward toward a clear portion of the sky (not too close to and never directly at the sun). There should be as few clouds as possible—preferably a completely clear sky.

3. Relax your gaze, while remaining mentally present and aware of the sky. After a few moments, or perhaps a few tries, tiny spark-like points of light should become visible, as if overlain atop the blurry background of the blue sky. They tend to swim like fish and move somewhat erratically.

4. The longer you can remain in this state of vision, the more accessible it will become.

Notes

Some have called these little points of light or sparks "little sprites," ascribing to them the status of tiny spirits of the air. A quasi-official scientific theory is that what is really being seen is blood cells moving in front of the eye's retina. I leave it to you to formulate your own theories, as the "answer," so to speak, is relatively unimportant to our purposes.

If you cannot access this state of vision or do not see the points of light the first time, keep trying and remember to remain relaxed. If this exercise either is something you are already familiar with or remains unsuccessful for you, skip to the next exercise, Seeing Inward.

EXERCISE: SEEING INWARD

This exercise will prepare you to see the inner layer of our personal ætheric energy—the radiant luminescence that shines a few inches outward from our physical body. Either sit approximately six to ten feet in front of a completely bare, light-colored wall or lie on a bed or floor facing upward toward a bare, light-colored ceiling. Remember, you should be able to do this relatively comfortably, since remaining relaxed is paramount.

Following these directions, I have included both a variation and an advanced version of the Seeing Inward exercise.

Directions

1. Extend your arm so that the back of your hand, palm open, is in your direct line of sight, fingers slightly apart. Bring your gaze to a space between two of your fingers and relax your vision—de-focus.

2. Keep your relaxed gaze and awareness on the space between two of your fingers.

3. After some time, a silver-white sliver of light outlining the edge of your finger or fingers should become visible. There may even appear to be a colored vapor-like haze just beyond this inner sliver. Do not re-focus your gaze on it to see it directly.

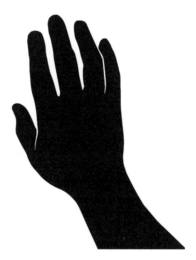

Hand in Front

Note

As mentioned earlier, these two types of vision will fuse with time and consistent practice. For now, you must strengthen your use of and access to this passive state of vision, as it develops in its early stages.

EXERCISE: SEEING INWARD VARIATION

This is a variation of the previous exercise that will help you better understand what is meant when we say to "become aware" of things in your field of vision without directly focusing your vision and looking directly at simple household objects such as pictures.

Directions
1. Sit comfortably in a chair about six to ten feet from a wall that has multiple things hanging on it or placed before it.
2. Relax your gaze to a stare, while remaining aware of the wall and objects upon it before you.
3. Without focusing your vision or looking directly at each object, keep your gaze relaxed and become aware of each individual object on or in front of the wall—perhaps first a picture, then a mirror, next a shelf or bookcase. In this same way, we may train ourselves to become aware of ætheric energy without looking directly at it.

EXERCISE: SEEING INWARD ADVANCED VARIATION

Place both hands five to ten inches in front of your face, as pictured in the diagram below. This exercise should be worked in the usual way—in front of a bare wall or ceiling. A piece of blank printer paper will also serve.

Hand and Finger Positions

Directions
1. Palms toward your face, hands relaxed, with fingers slightly spread, bring the tips of your middle fingers as close together as possible without touching.

2. Focus your relaxed gaze on the space between the tips of your two middle fingers and very slowly move them away from each other.

3. Repeat this exercise until the light of the ætheric energy becomes visible. You may see the inner layer of the ætheric double, as well as other lights that move like a cloudy haze or electrical pulses similar to those observed in a novelty plasma globe.

4. Feel free to improvise with hand and finger positions once the sight has been further developed by this practice.

EXERCISE: SEEING OTHERS

This exercise will accustom you to viewing someone else's ætheric field, which is a central aspect of developing ætheric sight. For this exercise, you may need a partner, or you can record yourself with either photo or video using a decent camera.

Directions

Either sit while recording yourself or have a partner sit about two to six feet in front of a blank, light-colored wall. There should be no obstructions between you and the person you are viewing—the subject.

1. Once you have achieved a state of relaxation, bring your relaxed gaze to a point just a few inches over the subject's shoulder, perhaps at the junction of the shoulder and neck.

2. Keep your gaze relaxed and become aware of the full luminescent radiance of the inner ætheric body appearing to radiate from the subject's physical form. It may present as a sliver of light at first, but becoming more relaxed while increasing awareness of it will typically allow the viewer to perceive it as its broader spectrum.

3. Gradually bring your awareness to the outer edges of the inner ætheric body and notice any changes in density and color.

Note

This exercise is further expanded by having the subject stand or move before a completely blank, light-colored wall while the viewer becomes aware of the colored light that radiates throughout the wider sphere of sensation.

Shoulder

PHASE 2: FEELING

Physical and tactile perception of ætheric energy is a significant aspect of the practice of ætheric magic. Not only does this sense allow the practitioner to confirm when energy is moving, but it also assists in familiarizing us with the nature of energy flow throughout the body and broader ætheric field. It can also help us diagnose blockages in the ætheric field of ourselves and others.

Ætheric energy has a very distinct sensation approximating an intense, but not uncomfortable, feeling of static electricity as well as the push-pull sensation, which will be familiar to anyone who has experimented with magnets before.

EXERCISE: FEELING THE ÆTHERIC

The following is a basic exercise that will assist you in feeling ætheric energy. Remember, it's important to remain completely relaxed before engaging in any attempt at feeling ætheric energy—similarly to the soft gaze necessary for ætheric sight, a soft touch and gentle body posture are necessary to begin to feel the fluid-like flow of the energy throughout the body.

Directions

1. Close your eyes, take a few deep breaths, and in a comfortable position, bring your hands together as if praying.

2. Rub them together somewhat vigorously for ten to twenty seconds. This friction will create heat and prepare the palm centers to give and receive energy.

3. Next, separate the hands about shoulder width apart, then slowly bring the palms as close together as possible without touching for about thirty seconds.

4. Slowly pull them away from each other to about shoulder width distance. Pay attention to and note any sensations. Experiment with doing this with eyes open and closed to see if one works better for you.

5. Repeat three to four times. Remember to remain relaxed and breathe deeply and slowly.

EXERCISE: FEELING SHAPES

This exercise and its variation will help you feel specific sensations that relate to the formation of shapes with the ætheric field. Your tactile sense will be trained to begin feeling contours, and you'll also begin to sense the relationships between the left and right hands, which we'll delve into in further detail. Remember to keep your shoulders, arms, and fingers relaxed during these exercises. Muscular and mental tension restrict the flow of ætheric energy and attenuate our perceptive abilities.

Directions

1. Close your eyes, take a few deep breaths, and in a comfortable position bring your hands before you to about chest height as if holding a ball.

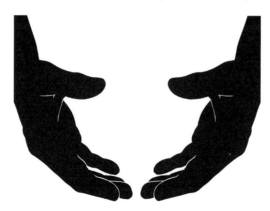

Light Ball

2. Keep your hands relaxed, fingers slightly apart with fingertips aligned but not touching.

3. Allow your intuition to gently adjust the size of this ball, but remain relaxed.

4. When you have established its size, tune in and try to sense and feel the ball.

5. Make note of any sensations or thoughts that arise.

6. Finish the exercise by dissolving the ball and rubbing your hands together vigorously.

EXERCISE: FEELING SHAPES VARIATION

This is a variation on the previous exercise.

Directions

1. Perform steps 1 though 3 of the previous Feeling Shapes exercise.

2. In your mind's eye, envision your hands gently holding a ball of pure white light. Allow your intuition to guide you to how big or small the ball should be.

3. Then open your eyes slowly and remain in this position. Keep your relaxed gaze on the space between the tips of your fingers. The sensation that should arise is one of soft, static electricity—a kind of buzzing feeling. The Projection and Reception Points in the center of your palms may even stimulate to activity and feel like a cool buzzing or whirling sensation.

4. At any point in this exercise, your arms may want to raise or lower themselves, almost as if invisibly pulled by a magnet. Lean into this and allow your body to move in whatever way it feels called, but keep your hands in the posture and remain relaxed.

EXERCISE: FEELING ENERGY ADVANCED

1. Standing in a comfortable position, close your eyes and take a few deep breaths.

2. Bring your hands in a cupped position up to your face, palms inward as pictured below.

3. Where your hands go, bring your awareness. This means trying to focus or become aware of that spot. When we do this, we begin to notice any tension—physical, mental, or emotional—associated with this anatomical area.

Hands to Face

4. Bring the centers of your palms into alignment with the third eye or Sulfur Center between the eyebrows and hold there while breathing deeply for roughly thirty seconds to a minute. It's perfectly fine to estimate, as needing to concentrate on counting may interfere with your ability to perceive any sensations.

5. Take note in this position of any images that arise in the eye of the mind.

6. Slowly lower your hands in a gentle, fluid motion to the Mercury Center at the midpoint of the chest, on the sternum.

7. Keep your hands and finger relaxed, breathing deeply for another thirty to sixty seconds.

8. Take note of any emotions that may stir, but take care not to let them overwhelm you.

9. Next, slowly bring the hands in a gentle and fluid motion down the center column to the Salt Center, just below the navel as pictured.

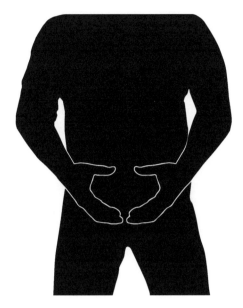

Salt Posture

10. Hold here in a relaxed state, continuing to breathe deeply for another thirty to sixty seconds, approximately.

11. Take note of any sensations, thoughts, or images that arise in this time.

12. From this position, which we will refer to as the Salt Posture, bring your hands and forearms with a gentle bend in the elbow out about ten to twelve inches at waist height, holding there for another thirty to sixty seconds, approximately. Over time, it is recommended that the practitioner extend the time spent in each position, as their ability to retain each position in a relaxed and comfortable state increases.

13. Close out as described at the beginning of the chapter.

EXERCISE: SCANNING THE SPHERE OF SENSATION

The following exercise is utilized as a diagnostic method to sense and locate any abnormalities or issues within a person's sphere of sensation, ætheric body, and physical body. This technique is derived from a practice called *byosen scanning*, which I learned during my initiations in the Japanese art of energy work, reiki. The sphere of sensation can be divided into four distinct layers, which have a direct relationship to the planes and bodies and to the four Qabalistic worlds.

It will be necessary to have a partner with whom to practice this technique until it is developed. Make sure this is someone you feel comfortable with and who feels comfortable with you, as you will need explicit and subconscious permission to enter their field (sphere of sensation). If there are subconscious resentments or ill feelings, the subject may subconsciously resist the exercise. This is an area where ethics and consent are paramount.

Directions

1. Have the subject comfortably lie down on their back and extend their arm out straight in front of them. This gives the practitioner an approximate sense of where the outermost boundary of the subject's sphere of sensation is. This layer corresponds to the spiritual body of the individual. To clarify—*it is not the spiritual body of the person* but corresponds to the energetic presence of the spiritual in their microcosm.

2. Once the outer layer of the sphere of sensation is approximated, have the subject lower their arm to rest at their side, and bring energy to your Projection and Reception Points in the hands. The Reception Point is typically the one most responsive to this technique, so I advise beginning with the receptive hand.

3. Once the hands are "awakened" and the practitioner can feel the almost electromagnetic charge, begin by slowly passing the hand over the outer boundary, palm down, from above the head down to below the soles of the feet. The practitioner may want to close their eyes to help focus more of their awareness in their tactile sense, or if ætheric sight has been sufficiently developed, they may use both in tandem.

4. Try to notice any deviations in sensation. This may indicate an irregularity corresponding to this layer of the psyche-ætheric organism. Take note of the quality of the sensation, as well as the location.

5. When this layer is complete, return the hand to above the head, about six inches lower than your previous pass. This layer corresponds to the mental body of the subject.

6. Complete a pass as before, stopping and making note at the location of any deviation in sensation. It may feel as if the energy is pulsing, stabbing, throbbing, or swirling and may also vary in temperature.

7. Return the hand to above the head another six inches lower than the previous pass, and complete a pass as usual. This layer corresponds to the astral body of the subject.

8. Finally, bring the hand to just above the top of the head, just barely touching their physical body. Make a pass once more in the usual manner, following all preceding protocols.

9. When finished, proceed to dry bathe, running the right hand from the top of the left shoulder to the right hip in a sweeping motion, then the left hand from the top of the right shoulder to the left hip in a sweeping motion. Next, extend the right arm and hand, fingers straight, palm facing up, and sweep the left arm with the right hand. Do the same for the right arm with the left hand. Imagine a discharge of any accumulated or transferred energies with these sweeping motions. End the dry bath with the quintessence posture.

Dry Bathing

1. Run the right hand from top of the left shoulder to the right hip in a sweeping motion.

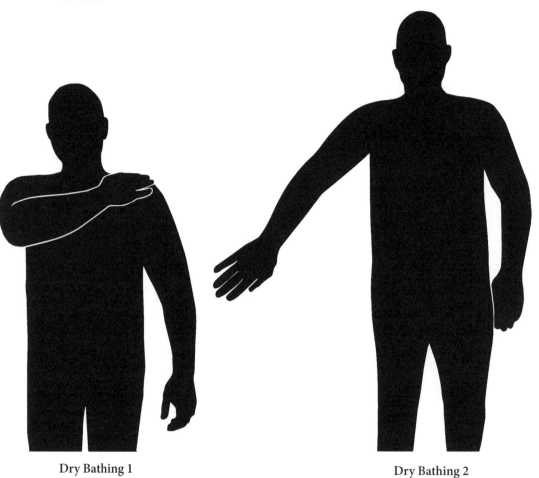

Dry Bathing 1   Dry Bathing 2

2. Then run the left hand from the top of the right shoulder to the left hip in a sweeping motion.

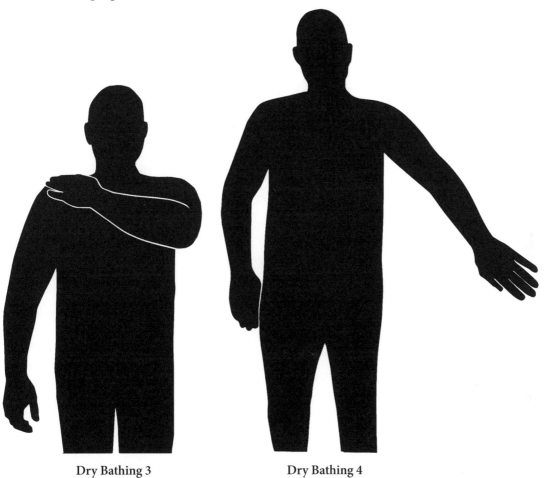

Dry Bathing 3   **Dry Bathing 4**

3. Extend the right arm and hand, fingers straight, palm facing up, and sweep the left arm with the right hand.

Dry Bathing 5

Dry Bathing 6

4. Do the same for the right arm with the left hand. Imagine a discharge of any accumulated or transferred energies with these sweeping motions.

5. End the dry bath with the quintessence posture.

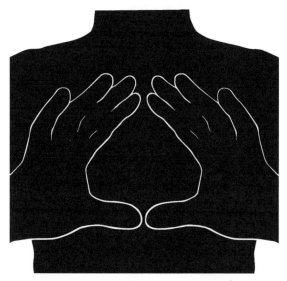

Quintessence Posture

Note

If after this you feel you have retained any unwanted energy from the exercise, take a bath with Epsom salts and ground, preferably with a meal of nuts and root vegetables.

PHASE 3: BREATHING

Breath work, as mentioned earlier, is essential to the linking and movement of ætheric energy through the body at the initial stages and remains a vital tool in later stages of development. Breath work can be combined with visualization to generate specific elemental qualities by conditioning ætheric energy. It can also help with directing energy in and out of the body.

All phase 3 exercises should be performed for the same amount of days, over the course of at least two weeks, before moving on to the next section.

EXERCISE: POWER BREATHING

The Power Breathing technique is practiced to develop the ability to release and draw in a specific type of elemental force. The following exercise is based on a technique given in the *Quareia Apprentice* module by Josephine McCarthy.[38] It is essentially an energy-on-demand technique.

The technique should be performed in the Deity-Form Posture in which you are seated in an upright position, either in a straight-backed chair or sitting erect on the edge of a seat or chair. Your feet should be placed firmly on the ground with knees at 90-degree angles, both feet and knees about hip-width apart. Your arms and shoulders should be relaxed, with hands resting atop the legs.

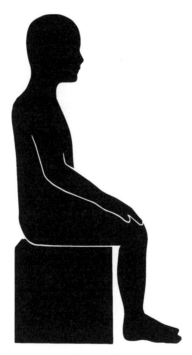

Deity-Form Posture

Directions

1. Sit in Deity-Form Posture and take a few deep, centering breaths while relaxing the body completely, with eyes closed.

2. Keep the microcosmic pathway posture. Your teeth should be gently touching, the tip of the tongue resting on the roof of the mouth, which typically occurs naturally when the mouth is closed.

---

38. Josephine McCarthy, *Quareia Apprentice* (UK: Quareia Publishing, 2016).

3. When deep, rhythmic breathing has been achieved, visualize yourself breathing in white smoke tinged with gold sparkles. Pull this light down into the Salt Center with the breath.

4. Exhale slowly, visualizing a gray smoke being blown out through the mouth, completely leaving your body to be reabsorbed into the ætheric field. This smoke represents physical, mental, and emotional toxins.

5. After a few rounds of this, bring the left hand up to the left nostril, pressing it closed with the index and ring finger. This is called moon breath. On the inhalation, visualize pulling in red smoke through the right nostril, and pull this down with the breath into the Mercury Center, where it will be stored. On the exhalation, breathe out the gray smoke.

6. After a few rounds of this, release the left nostril, bringing the left hand back to Deity-Form Posture position, and close the right nostril with the right hand by the same method. This is called sun breath.

7. Breathe in blue smoke through the left nostril, pulling it down to the Mercury Center and storing it there, where it blends with the red smoke. Breathe out the gray smoke.

8. End the exercise with a few deep breaths out of both nostrils.

EXERCISE: BREATHING THE ÆTHER

As mentioned in the section on the elements in chapter 5, elemental air—inclusive of breath—has an intimate affinity with ætheric energy. Air was thought to carry the rays of the sun and moon, which were associated with ætheric energy in primeval shamanic traditions. Systems of energy work that emerged from these traditions utilize a term that simultaneously meant "energy" and "breath" (i.e., prana, qi, ruach, pneuma, etc.). Conscious attention to and control of the breath will help the practitioner begin linking their personal ætheric energy to their conscious mind, as we will use the breath as a device to begin training the mind to focus on the movement of energy in sensation and visualization.

Directions

1. In a seated position, take a few deep, rhythmic breaths, keeping your teeth gently touching, so that your mouth is gently closed.

2. Place your hands palm down on your abdomen just below your navel and continue drawing in the breath by expanding the abdomen and diaphragm, exhaling slowly through the nostrils.

3. Notice the breath as it moves through your airways as your abdomen slowly rises and falls, feeling the ebb and flow of your body.

4. Inhale, bringing your awareness to your Salt Center as your abdomen fills with breath, then bring awareness to your nostrils while you exhale.

5. Visualize the Middle Pillar filling with light on each inhalation and the Salt Center filling with this light, where it gathers like a radiant elixir.

6. Repeat for a number of repetitions before closing out.

7. Note any thoughts, sensations, or feelings that arise in your journal.

PHASE 4: MOVEMENT

In many modalities of energy work and healing, movement is thought of as medicine. Movement is as expressive as any other facet of an individual of interior states. Lethargic and heavy movements indicate similar and related earthy and watery qualities within an individual's psyche-ætheric landscape. Quick and uncoordinated movements indicate imbalances of elemental air and fire. Excesses and blockages can occur, and an essential part of the ætheric magic practitioner's personal praxis is in the maintenance of the health and harmonized flow of ætheric energy throughout their body and ætheric field. This facilitates power, awareness, an accumulation of æther, and healthy movement of æther, which can be readily employed for any number of magical purposes. It also contributes to the general good health of the practitioner.

Movement can also be regarded as a flavor of expression that prompts or commands ætheric energy to manifest or move in a specific way or through a specific pathway. These movements and postures serve to ergonomically move ætheric energy in organic directions through its natural pathways in the body. You'll learn more about this in the section on postures in chapter 8, on techniques of ætheric magic. The next series of exercises will involve the application of postures, movements, breath work, and visualization. These exercises are also meant to generate a state similar to standing meditation, and, as an aside, having a meditative practice of some kind will be of immense value to this curriculum and magic in general. All the following exercises should be ended by closing out.

It will be necessary at first to establish a firm connection between the breath and the various alchemical centers by way of the Middle Pillar or channel of energy movement along the centerline of your body. The kind of breath we will be using is diaphragmatic and employs a technique of drawing in breath with the diaphragm and expansion of the belly, rather than strictly costal or chest breathing.

EXERCISE: PREPARING THE MIDDLE PILLAR POSTURE

At this point, you'll be assuming total body postures, the first of which we'll call Middle Pillar Posture. This posture will be our starting point for every exercise and technique going forward. It represents a relaxed, rooted, and upright starting position, from which the practitioner can move with the minimum amount of effort while maintaining a balanced, supportive posture.

Directions

1. To start off, your feet should be parallel, about shoulder width apart.

2. Bend your knees slightly. Locked knees will inhibit movement of ætheric energy around the body.

3. Your hips should be slightly thrust forward to lengthen and slightly straighten the spine and to prevent excess curvature in the lower spine.

4. Your shoulders should be in line with the ears while remaining completely relaxed. Arms should be relaxed at your sides, and the neck should be relaxed, with the sensation that the head is gently balanced atop it.

5. Your chin should be slightly tucked in toward the neck, without any discomfort. It should feel as if you are a marionette and there is a string attached to the crown of your head, gently pulling it slightly upward.

6. Your teeth should be gently touching, with your tongue in resting position, which will typically mean that the tip of the tongue is touching the forward part of the palate (roof of mouth).

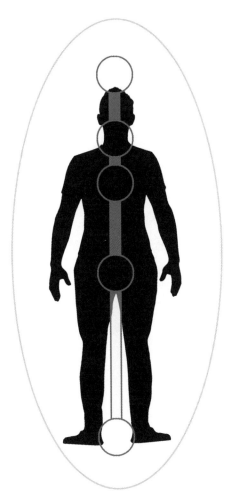

Middle Pillar Posture

7. It is important to note that your breathing should be rhythmic (symmetrical), deep, diaphragmatic breath work. Synching your breath to the visualization of the movement of ætheric energy is *the key* to linking our minds to it, bringing it under conscious control, rather than a mere matter-of-fact mechanism of the movement of energy. The end goal is to be able to move ætheric energy independent of our breathing patterns.

Middle Pillar Posture Side View

EXERCISE: UNITING ABOVE AND BELOW

The following exercise, referred to as Uniting Above and Below, is an opening and preparation for the work in its own right. You will activate the central pathway of ætheric energy as well as consciousness—Middle Pillar. We have five modes or centers, which exemplify the different aspects or qualities this energy takes on in different centers of the body, which are associated with different functions and types of consciousness associated at each respective location. These are further grouped into the three alchemical centers, which enable us to locate specific anatomical centers associated with the accumulation of ætheric energy by time-tested observation in lineages of traditional medicine. Once they are located, we can work with these anatomical energetic centers the same way we would work with any other system in the body (be it cardiorespiratory, lymphatic, etc.) to move energy through specific pathways.

In order to begin pulling in and moving ætheric energy from the exterior environment (the macrocosm) into and around the sphere of sensation, you will need to identify and work with opening and closing specific access points, which are the Earth Root Points and the Crown Point at the crown of your head. In this exercise, you will use these points to draw in earthly and celestial forms of æther to empower and vitalize the personal ætheric field/sphere of sensation—kind of like putting fuel in a vehicle.

Directions

1. Start by assuming Middle Pillar Posture. Then, with a few deep, rhythmic breaths, perform a quick mental body scan to assess where you are holding tension and release it with a deep exhalation.

2. After a few more deep, centering breaths, bring your awareness to the Earth Root Points on the soles of your feet. Imagine these points as swirling with activity. This kind of visualization is called *opening the point*.

3. When the Earth Root Points are opened, imagine deep roots digging down into the earth, deeper with each full breath.

4. After a few breaths, raise the energy of celestial salt from the deep, dark earth, bringing it up through the roots, up the Middle Pillar to the Salt Center in the lower abdomen and upper pelvic area, storing it there as a glowing, bright white elixir. Feel it rooting and grounding you.

5. Repeat this three times.

6. After you have filled the cauldron of salt with the elixir of celestial salt, bring your awareness to your Spirit Crown Point and open it to activity.

7. Once opened, imagine a large cone of light there, like a crown, reaching up toward the sky. On the inhalation, pull down the energy of celestial niter

from the sun and stars. Let it enter through the Spirit Crown Point and accumulate in the Sulfur Center, inside the cranium, behind the point of the third eye. Feel the energy enlivening and energizing you.

8. Do this three times and then gently bring your awareness to the Mercury Center, encompassing the center of the chest cavity and the solar plexus in the upper abdomen.

9. On an exhalation, visualize the roots reaching deeper into darkest earth, while the crown of light reaches up higher toward the sky; on the inhalation, pull in energy from both directions simultaneously, having them meet at the Mercury Center, blending and mixing, uniting the whole and establishing the Middle Pillar of Light.

10. Do this three times, slowly, following your deep, rhythmic breathing patterns, and then remain in Middle Pillar Posture for a few moments before visualizing the Earth Rooting Points and Spirit Crown Point, closing down, and the roots and crown fading from view.

11. Circulate the energy through the sphere of sensation through the Middle Pillar with the overhead circular clearing movement we used in the sealing the circuit exercise starting on page 65, and then close out.

12. Bring your awareness gently back to the room in which you are, and end the exercise with some light stretching if needed.

EXERCISE: UNITING ABOVE AND BELOW VARIATION

A further elaboration of this exercise entails the sequential visualization of the sephiroth of the Middle Pillar of the Tree of Life from Kether to Malkuth, or the sephiroth of the entire Tree of Life in the sphere of sensation also visualized sequentially, as pictured on the next page. This variation helps us expand our network of ætheric channels and power centers beyond the dantian and home in on the sephirothic centers, which give expanded access to various forces and essences within our sphere of sensation.

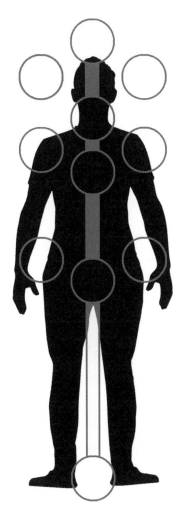

The Sephiroth over the Sphere of Sensation

EXERCISE: THREE CENTERS DISTILLATION

In this exercise, we will be moving through a series of postures again beginning with the Middle Pillar Posture.

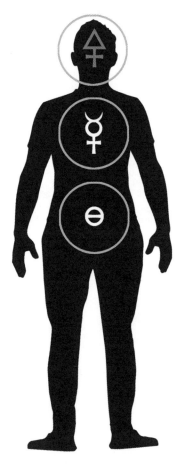

Tria Prima Centers

Directions

1. Assume Middle Pillar Posture and perform the United Above and Below exercise.

2. Then, raise the arms to a circular position at the vale of the chest, as if holding a very large ball up to your chest, bringing the tips of the middle fingers together and almost but not quite touching as in previous exercises.

3. Imagine the ætheric energy in your Mercury Center circulating from your chest through your arms and hands in one big circuit, traveling in the direction of what you have discerned to be the hand of projection.

4. Circulate the energy here, while keeping your upper back, shoulders, arms, and hands as relaxed as possible for a few moments. This is the Mercury Posture.

Mercury Posture

5. Next, slowly raise the arms and hands upward in front of your forehead, forming a kind of triangle there with your index fingers and thumbs (palms facing away from your face) so that the Third Eye Point between the brows is

directly centered in the triangle your hands are making. Experiment with the distance between this point and your hands.

6. Feel the energy of the Third Eye Point become stimulated and picture a white ball of light (approximately eight inches in diameter) forming between your hands. This is the Sulfur Posture.

Sulfur Posture

7. Finally, holding this glowing ball of brilliant white light, slowly lower your arms and hands to the point just below and in front of the navel. Become aware of the elixir glowing ever brighter with each inhalation and not dimin-

ishing on the exhalation, taking in the energy of this ball of white light. This is Salt Posture.

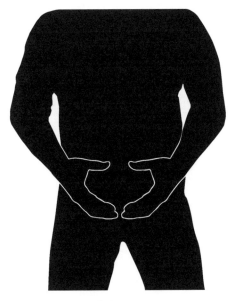

Salt Posture

8. After a few moments, resume Middle Pillar Posture, and after a few breaths, close out and end the exercise as usual.

EXERCISE: CONTROL OF THE SPHERE OF SENSATION

The following exercise serves to develop conscious control and maintain the health of the sphere of sensation. It consists of expanding and contracting the sphere of sensation and making it more or less permeable.

1. Visualize the sphere of sensation in its entirety, with no gaps or holes in it, radiating a bright golden light.
2. With an exhalation, see the sphere of sensation expand to twice its size, encompassing anything that might be within that space. Hold this visualization for a few moments (the breath does not need to be held).
3. On an inhalation, bring the sphere of sensation back to normal size (about an arms length in all directions).

4. Visualize the sphere of sensation becoming thinner and porous, more permeable. Take note of any thoughts, sensations, or feelings.

5. Visualize the sphere of sensation becoming completely solidified to the point where the outer boundary is between three to six inches thick.

6. Repeat these variations several times and make a note of any associated thoughts, sensations, and feelings in your journal.

EXERCISE: THE ALEMBIC

The Alembic is a strengthening and vitalizing of the outer boundary of the sphere of sensation and a pouring in of ætheric energy in its most spiritual (unconditioned elementally) form for uses of empowering, charging, and healing. This exercise will be performed while either standing in Middle Pillar Posture or seated in what we will call Deity-Form Posture.

1. After a few deep breaths with eyes closed, imagine a sphere of bright white light forming at the location of your Malkuth Center, the upper half encompassing the tops of your feet, and the lower half descending into the ground below, anchoring you.

2. Feel the sphere of light permeating the physical area of your body in which it is located, infusing your musculature with a comfortable level of warmth and deep relaxation.

3. Once you have achieved relaxation, inhale, slowly raising the sphere up the legs, easing all tension in every muscle and joint, finally bringing it to the Yesod Center (pelvis/lower abdomen), pausing there for a few breaths to feel it there. Make a note of any thoughts, feelings, or emotions that arise.

4. Slowly move the sphere up the torso to the Tiphareth Center (center chest/upper abdomen), stopping there for a few breaths. Everywhere the sphere of light goes, tension—whether physical, mental, or emotional—cannot persist, and a calm state of relaxation takes its place, filling your body with a soothing bright white light.

5. Bring the sphere up to the Da'ath Center (neck/mouth), then Kether Center (third eye/crown of head) in the same manner.

6. After a few moments, take another deep breath, and on exhaling, see the ætheric light rush upward and out of your Spirit Crown Point like a foundation of fiery water, slowly raining down around your sphere of sensation.

7. Do this three times and collect the light of the ætheric energy once again into a sphere at your Malkuth Center (feet/ground). On an inhalation, see the light there turn into a whirl, like multiple strands of ribbon, winding upward around the outer boundary of your sphere of sensation, enveloping you completely.

8. For a few breaths, sit inside this solid egg-shaped container of ætheric light in which you have enveloped yourself, feeling its brightness penetrate your entire body, energizing you, restoring you, bringing healing and power.

9. On an exhalation, see the light unwrap itself back into ribbons, gently falling back to the sphere of light at your Malkuth Center.

10. After doing this a total of three times, center the energy in your Tiphareth Center by way of the Middle Pillar, close out, and gradually bring your awareness back to the room you are in.

EXERCISE: HARMONIZING THE ELEMENTS

In this exercise, you will utilize the Middle Pillar Posture (posture only—not the full exercise) as a preliminary and use the visualization of the five sephiroth of the Middle Pillar, from lowest to uppermost: Malkuth (feet/ground), Yesod (pelvis/lower abdomen), Tiphareth (center chest/upper abdomen), Da'ath (neck/mouth), and Kether (third eye/crown of head—should be visualized in a similar way as a crown would sit atop the head). To these sephiroth, we will attribute various elemental colors, and each will represent a particular element. There are several possible attributions to each, but we will utilize the following:

Malkuth: Black (earth)
Yesod: Blue (water)
Tiphareth: White (spirit)
Da'ath: Yellow (air)
Kether: Red (fire)

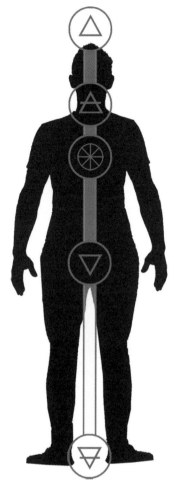

Elemental Middle Pillar

This attribution of the elements is selected with a mind to the view of alchemical mercury being regarded as the spirit principle of the philosophical essentials of the Tria Prima and as the mediating principle, which occupies a central, unifying position.

When performing this exercise, it is important to view these elements as transforming into one another, which will be indicated by the changing colors of the beam of light. However, the elemental Middle Pillar can just as easily be worked by switching the attributions of fire and spirit, making Kether the spirit center and Tiphareth the fire center. Experimentation will help determine which attributions you prefer, and each can be used for different purposes.

Directions

1. After a few breaths, visualize a beam of bright white light descending from the divine immensity far beyond the furthest reaches of the cosmos, reaching you at the sphere of your Kether Center (crown of head), which glows a primary red color.

2. Visualize a fire triangle at the center of this sphere and watch it grow brighter with each breath.

3. After a few moments, watch the beam of now red light descend to a sphere at your Da'ath Center (base of neck), colored a primary yellow.

4. Visualize an air triangle in the center of the sphere and watch it glow brighter with each breath for several turns.

5. Next, bring the beam of now yellow light down through the Tiphareth Center (center of chest), down to rest at a sphere in the Yesod Center (pelvic area), colored a primary blue and inscribed with a water triangle at its center. Breathe in the same manner, envisioning the sphere growing brighter and brighter.

6. Then, visualize the beam of now blue light descending down to a black sphere at your Malkuth Center (feet/ground), inscribed with a white earth triangle at its center. With each breath, watch the white triangle glow brighter and brighter.

7. Finally, on the inhalation, bring the beam of bright white brilliance up to a sphere at your Tiphareth Center and envision a black spirit wheel inscribed at its center.

8. Gently bring your hands together to a position at the chest, with the tips of your fingers gently touching, forming a triangle centered on this sphere. This is the Quintessence Posture.

9. Breathe the light you have accumulated into the rest of the spheres, watching them glow brighter and brighter, until all the spheres on the Middle Pillar are completely white.

10. At this point, become aware of the light entered in your Tiphareth sphere and lower your arms slowly to rest at your sides.

11. Close out.

12. Take a few deep breaths, and bring your awareness gently back to the room you are in.

EXERCISE: THE ELEMENTAL CIRCUITS

Earlier in this book, I demonstrated how each finger corresponds to a particular element. You also adopted certain hand positions (i.e., *mudras* in the Vedic system; *jiuziyin* in the Taoist system) as part of your postures. These hand positions can be used to create elemental "circuits" of energy, to bring greater available concentration of these energies. Their application is simple.

Directions

1. In the Sulfur Posture, keep the tips of the thumbs (spirit) and ring fingers (fire) gently touching to complete the lesser circuit of fire.

Sulfur Posture/Fire Circuit

2. In the Salt Posture, keep the tips of the thumbs and index fingers (water) gently touching to complete the lesser circuit of water.

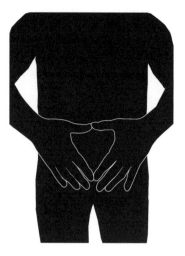

Salt Posture/Water Circuit

3. In the Quintessence Posture, keep the tips of the thumbs and little fingers (air) gently touching to complete the lesser circuit of air.

Quintessence Posture/Air Circuit

Or keep the tips of the thumbs gently touching and interlace the other fingers with the hands pressed gently up against the Mercury Center to create the diamond circuit. This posture can also be referred to as Stone Posture.

Stone Posture

Note

This exercise can be accompanied by any of the sound, vibration, and color visualizations given earlier.

EXERCISE: ALCHEMICAL CIRCULATIONS

The Alchemical Circulation involves the bringing in and movement of ætheric energy by way of rhythmic breathing and the visualization of white light as we have done in previous exercises. The following three exercises are useful in charging the sphere of sensation and Middle Pillar for higher amplitude ritual and healing work.

Directions: The Macrocosmic Orbit

1. Stand in Middle Pillar Posture or sit in Deity-Form Posture, taking deep rhythmic breaths connecting the microcosmic pathway while your eyes are closed.

2. Perform the Uniting Above and Below exercise (see page 92).

3. After centering the energy in your Mercury Center, bring the light up to the Sulfur Center, and on the exhalation, watch it fountain out of your Spirit Crown Point, descending back down around the sphere of sensation like a shower of white-golden sparks, collecting in a sphere at your feet.

4. On an inhalation, bring this stream of light up the back of the sphere of sensation to the Spirit Crown Point.

5. On an exhalation, bring this stream of light down the front of the sphere of sensation back down to the sphere at your feet. Do this several times.

6. Bring the stream of light up through the Middle Pillar to your Spirit Crown Point, and on the exhalation, move it down the left side of the sphere of sensation.

7. On the inhalation, bring the stream of light up the right side of the sphere of sensation.

8. Move the light up through the Middle Pillar, and gather the light in your Mercury Center.

Directions: The Microcosmic Orbit

1. Move the light to your Salt Center, gathering it there with several breaths. It is important to maintain the microcosmic pathway connection while performing this circulation.

2. Circulate the stream of light here through the microcosmic pathway, directing it down through the perineum and up the back to the Spirit Crown Point on an inhalation, where it descends on an exhalation down the centerline of the body, making one full orbit. The energy moved here should be visualized as being about the width of a pencil and running just beneath the skin. Do this for several repetitions.

3. Gather the light in the Salt Center once more, and then direct it out of a point about two inches below the navel, circulating it counterclockwise around the hips like a belt with the same visualization of width and depth as the previous circulation. Do this for several repetitions before absorbing it back into the Salt Center through the point below the navel.

Directions: The Vortex

1. Standing or seated, inhale and visualize the light coiling upward in a counterclockwise motion *around* the Middle Pillar, rather than through it.

2. Collect the energy at the Spirit Crown Point, and exhaling, visualize this coil of light spiraling downward in a clockwise spiral around the Middle Pillar.

3. Circulate the energy in this way for a few repetitions before gathering in the Sulfur Center.

EXERCISE: THE LIGHTNING FLASH AND SERPENT

This exercise is yet another alchemical circulation. It will utilize our Qabalistic Tree of Life system, as visualized in the sphere of sensation, and corresponds to various areas of the body. For acuity of visualization, the practitioner should familiarize themselves with the full diagram of the Lightning Flash and Serpent of Wisdom on the Tree of Life (see below), taking note of the location of the paths and the movement of the serpent.

Directions

1. Stand in Middle Pillar Posture and establish a visualization of the Tree of Life in the sphere of sensation.

2. Visualize your Kether Center radiant with bright white light. Then see a beam project downward toward you from the divine immensity in the beyond.

3. See this beam contact your Kether Center, sending a flash of light down the sphere of sensation through each of the sephiroth in the sphere of sensation, in time with an exhalation. This should resemble a flash of lightning.

4. Gather the light at your Malkuth Center, and with a slow inhalation, see the light wind up the path of the Serpent of Wisdom until it reaches your Kether Center.

5. Then see the light descend in another flash of lightning through the sephiroth.

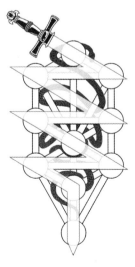

Lightning Flash and Serpent of Wisdom

6. Circulate the light in this way several times before gathering and centering it in the Tiphareth Center through the Middle Pillar.

OTHER POSTURES

In performing any of the exercises of circulation, breath work, visualization, and cultivation of ætheric energy, several other postures may be appropriately employed. A few good examples are the postures assumed by gods as depicted in Egyptian hieroglyphics, from which we get our Deity-Form Posture. The postures assumed by the figures of the major arcana of the tarot are also excellent for this usage. Following are two examples: the Magician and Temperance.

Magician Posture

Temperance Posture

Experiment for yourself with moving energy around the body and the greater sphere of sensation in these postures and note any thoughts, sensations, and feelings you have.

EXERCISE: CHARGING THE POINTS AND CENTERS

To stimulate particular centers into conscious activity, simply use the visualization and breath techniques along with the basic postures (Middle Pillar Posture, Salt Posture, Sulfur Posture, Mercury Posture, Quintessence Posture) to bring energy to a desired center in preparation for any kind of magical or healing work. Some measure of friction or physical blood flow to the area will assist in this as well (as in rubbing the hands together to activate the Reception and Projection Points) if visualization and breath work are not forthcoming in a timely manner. Here is an exercise on awakening and charging the Projection and Reception Points of the hands:

Directions

1. Assume Middle Pillar Posture.

2. Taking a few deep breaths, raise your hands in front of you as if you are about to clap.

3. Hold your hands about two inches apart at the palms, keeping your fingers relaxed.

4. Take a few deep, controlled breaths and bring your awareness to the space between your palms. What do you feel there?

5. After a few moments, pull your hands away from each other. Then clap them together strongly (without inflicting any pain on yourself) and rub them together, creating friction between the two—like rubbing two sticks together to create a fire. Do this for about thirty seconds and then stop.

6. Pull your hands away from each other and reposition them as they were at the second step of the exercise (two inches apart from palm to palm).

7. Bring your awareness back to the space between your palms and gently tune in to any sensations there. There may be heat, there may be a tingling—all or any of these are a good indication the points are charged and ready for your working.

TROUBLESHOOTING AND ADAPTING

What if you can't see ætheric energy or have other limitations that will affect your approach to the postures, gestures, and techniques of ætheric magic? There are methods of troubleshooting and adapting to these challenges that may make you an even better magician.

If you are still having trouble seeing ætheric energy, one technique is to assure yourself of its presence and imagine it. There may also be some other way in which you are able to sense the ætheric field. Experimentation and keeping a good record in your journal will help facilitate your understanding of the ways in which you uniquely sense ætheric energy. For instance, if you notice that at a certain point you feel a sensation like goose bumps, or maybe a more subtle sensation like detecting a slight elevation in the clarity of your awareness, or an ineffable interconnectedness to your immediate environment—these are all ways in which you could be becoming aware of and tuning in to the ætheric field.

If your particular circumstances require you to customize any of the postures or other techniques in this book, I recommend a similar adaptation. Tune in to your body at a greater depth—connect with the rhythms of your breathing and try to otherwise sense or imagine the energy moving in each particular circuit. Again, personal experimentation in this vein and keeping a detailed journal will help you paint your own picture of how the ætheric magic system will work for you.

CONCLUSION

In the course of these exercises, we have engaged our ætheric energy, beginning to sense it and bring it under conscious control with attention, perception, breath work, visualization, and intention in an effort to cultivate and direct it. In the process, we have also worked with the Middle Pillar sephiroth on the Tree of Life, the dyad of celestial salt and celestial niter, the alchemical Tria Prima, and the four elements with the quintessence of spirit. I have included an appendix of all postures for your easy reference. The distinction between the elemental division of the Middle Pillar and the alchemical is that the elemental pertains to permutation and balance of energies, whereas the Tria Prima, while also utilized in energetic balance, are specifically related to function. You've also perhaps unexpectedly learned how to move and channel ætheric energy in ways that are beneficial to clearing out stagnant accumulations, clearing blockages, and redirecting flow. Each of these exercises is a rudimentary preparation for magical operations and will be elaborated on in the next chapter.

You are now ready to begin working ætheric magic and projecting energy outside of your sphere of sensation. However, before you do that, let's take a look at a few other ways to cultivate and empower your sphere of sensation and magical efficacy in ætheric magic.

CHAPTER 7
SOUND, COLOR, AND TEMPERATURE

Three particular magical forces that I have not covered in detail yet are utilized by the magic practitioner in the system of ætheric magic. These are sound, color, and temperature, which are to be employed at various times in ritual and energetic exercises to activate various centers and stimulate and direct their associated kinds of ætheric energy. Sounds, colors, and temperature are specifically physical forces, as distinct from metaphysical forces such as those active on the astral level of creation—they act immediately upon physical matter and beings by vibrations conceived of scientifically as waves. Light therapy involving the use of different types of light on the color spectrum is used in the treatment of various illnesses and pathologies, including jaundice (blue light) and muscle soreness and recovery (red light). Sound therapy is used to mitigate stress and anxiety and increase focus. Temperature therapy such as ice bathing is used for autonomic nervous system regulation, while sauna treatments are used for detoxification.

In magic, these forces are brought together like a symphony by various implements and methods, in order to induce and cultivate within the practitioner's sphere of sensation a vivid and precise state corresponding to universal creative essences. In other words, you could craft a ritual invocation based on the specific colors, sounds, and temperatures corresponding to the elements, planets, and zodiacal signs, as well as the Tria Prima of salt, sulfur, and mercury. Let's look at some of these concepts in a little more detail.

SOUND

Sound is something considered sacred almost universally by magicians. It is conceived as being our microcosmic portion of the primordial power that creative Deity used to fashion the universe—vibration. According to nearly all ancient canons of magic both

East and West, the universe was created from a divine utterance, and the letters of the respective ancient scriptural alphabets were sacred symbols of these divine creative powers. In the Western musical scale, there is a system referred to as the *diatonic scale*, composed of seven tones or musical notes in sequence. To these seven notes that compose a musical scale is added an *octave*, or eighth and final note, which is the same as the first note of the scale at a higher pitch. This scale can be further broken down into incremental tonal progressions totaling in twelve musical notes from tonic (first note) to octave (first note at a higher pitch), referred to as the *chromatic scale*. The division of seven and twelve finds itself also in the classical planets and the zodiac.

Magical practitioners use sound, an energy released by something's vibrations, to awaken a particular aspect of the greater cosmic ætheric field. With a concentrated vibratory force focused and directed by will, clear visualization, and strong intention, a magical practitioner may effect a resonance similar to that which a tuning fork has on another object with a shared resonant frequency. Vibration of divine names and words of power usually takes the form of a deep, diaphragmatic intoning with a symmetrical rhythm. Depending on the vertical location of a particular center, with which divine names, words of power, and sounds are associated, different pitches may be used (higher at vertical top, lower at bottom). A key sign that the vibration is being performed effectively is feeling a certain movement in the area of the body related to the center whose names, words, and sound you are vibrating.

Aside from divine names associated with the sephiroth in Hermetic Qabalah and various pantheons of deities, there are three sounds we will employ in our system of ætheric magic. These correspond to the three mother letters mentioned earlier—aleph, mem, and shin. Shin corresponds to the Sulfur Center, and its sound is vibrated as *shhh*. Aleph corresponds to the Mercury Center, and its sound is vibrated as *ahhh*. Mem corresponds to the Salt Center, and its sound is vibrated as *mmmm*. These sounds are the three mother sounds; they are the vibratory expressions of the Tria Prima. The effects of their vibrations can be felt in the various parts of the human anatomy with which they are correlated.

As I mentioned earlier, ætheric magic practitioners utilize a chain of flow in ritual work that involves invocation, evocation, and consecration. This chain of flow is accessed primarily by the vibration of divine names, and it also corresponds to the Four Qabalistic Worlds. Essentially, we are attempting to pull or draw a particular force, entity, or energy down into our sphere of sensation and then fix it to a material object, such as a talisman. The Qabalistic World that corresponds to physical manifestation is the world of Assiah. Our physical ritual work is performed in Malkuth of Assiah, which literally translated is the "realm of making." To ground the current of force we stimulate and attempt to draw down to effect some kind of physical manifestation, gestures, words, and sounds are important. They represent a physical action symbolic of the process of drawing down power through the chain of flow and are one rationale for ritual work on the whole. Oftentimes a "rap," "knock," or "battery" is used in order to physically ground these energies and affirm that it has indeed been accomplished. This note may stimulate useful insights further on in our examination of magic as a kind of ætheric circuitry.

EXERCISE: SOUNDING THE CENTERS

This exercise will be split into two versions and will focus on helping you use sound to activate vibrations in specific areas of your body, which, as we have seen, correspond to specific actions and aspects of your human organism. You'll first be using the Tria Prima power centers in version one of this exercise and then the sephirothic system of the Qabalistic Middle Pillar in version two. It may be helpful to have an audio or video recording of these exercises so that you can keep track of the pitches.

Directions: The Tria Prima Power Centers

1. Assume Middle Pillar Posture and take a few deep, centering breaths. Keep your teeth gently touching with your tongue at rest.

2. Visualize the three power centers of the Tria Prima along your centerline: the Sulfur Center in your cranial cavity, the Mercury Center in your chest cavity, and the Salt Center in your lower abdominal cavity.

3. Begin by humming—no specific note, just hum—and observe where the vibration of your humming can be felt in your body. This may take some experimentation. Try humming lower and higher, and take note of any bodily sensation no matter how minute.

4. Raise the pitch of your humming until you can feel vibration in your head—teeth, tongue, forehead, etc. Try to find the pitch where the vibration is most intense in your face or head.

5. Continue humming as you zero in on the center of your head and visualize the Sulfur Center stimulating to activity, glowing a scintillating white. Continue this for as long as it feels appropriate.

6. Take a few deep breaths and again begin humming, this time lowering your pitch until you can feel vibration in your chest. This should be a little more appreciable since the chest is a bigger cavity and contains the organs you are using to vibrate (diaphragm, lungs).

7. Focus on the feeling of vibration in your chest and visualize the Mercury Center stimulating to activity, glowing a scintillating white. Continue this for as long as it feels appropriate.

8. Take a few deep breaths and now vibrate at a low tone. Try to feel the tone vibrating as low down in your torso as possible. Not everyone has a broad enough vocal range to get their lower abdomen to vibrate at first, but get the hum as low as you can without it breaking up.

9. Focus in on this low vibration and visualize your Salt Center stimulating to activity, glowing a scintillating white, for as long as it feels appropriate.

10. Take a few deep breaths and close out.

Directions: The Middle Pillar Spheres

1. Assume Middle Pillar Posture and take a few deep breaths. Keep your teeth gently touching and your tongue at rest.

2. Visualize the sephirotic centers along the Middle Pillar of your centerline within your body.

3. Begin by humming in the same manner as the previous variation of this exercise to find the pitch at which you begin to feel vibrations in the center of your head.

4. Once this vibration is established, intone (sing) this note loudly, trying to feel the vibration there.

5. Visualize your Kether Center (crown of head) stimulating to activity, glowing a scintillating white. Sound this note for as long as it takes for you to strongly envision your Kether Center completely radiant.

6. Take a few deep breaths and close your mouth so that your teeth are gently touching again, with your tongue at rest.

7. Begin humming again and find the pitch with which you can feel vibration in your neck and throat.

8. Sing this note and visualize your Da'ath Center (nape of neck) glowing a scintillating white. Do this for as long as it takes for you to strongly envision your Da'ath Center completely radiant.

9. Take a few deep breaths and close your mouth again, teeth touching and tongue at rest.

10. Hum the pitch with which vibration can be felt in the center of the chest.

11. Sing/intone this pitch, feeling the vibration in your chest and visualizing your Tiphareth Center (center of chest) glowing a scintillating white. Do this for as long as it takes to see this center completely radiant.

12. Take a few deep breaths and close your mouth again, teeth gently touching, tongue at rest.

13. Hum at the pitch with which vibration can be felt in the lower abdomen or the lowest part of your torso.

14. Visualize your Yesod Center (lower abdomen and pelvis) glowing a scintillating white. Do this for as long as it takes for you to strongly envision this center completely radiant.

15. Take a few deep breaths and close your mouth, teeth gently touching with your tongue at rest.

16. Hum as low as you possibly can. Find the pitch that is at the complete lowest end of your vocal range.

17. Sing/intone this note. It may not feel very strong, since vibrations at this end of the spectrum of sound have longer sine wave oscillations and therefore are not very prominent to human ears.

18. Visualize your Malkuth Center (feet and ground) glowing a scintillating white. Do this for as long as it takes for you to envision this center completely radiant.

19. Take a few deep breaths and close out.

EXERCISE: THE UNIVERSAL VOICE

For some practitioners, it may be entirely impractical or completely impossible to vibrate or intone words and names out loud for various reasons. In this instance, they may use the universal voice.

Directions

1. When it is necessary to vibrate a Divine Name or Word of Power, visualize that name or word glowing with either white brilliance or an appropriate corresponding color for the force to be employed in your Mercury/Tiphareth Center.

2. In vision, without making any audible sound, see yourself vibrating the name or word and the light leaving your Mercury/Tiphareth Center, being projected into the furthest reaches of the universe.

3. See it vibrate the very foundations of the landscape, and know that it has reached its destination and performed its goal.

COLOR

Each of these sounds and centers is associated with a particular color. In fact, the seven colors of the rainbow correspond to the seven tones of the Western musical scale. Color, like sound, is an extremely powerful tool in the magical tool kit of a practitioner. Color is also a manifestation or expression of vibratory energy and can have tremendous effects on consciousness and physical, mental, and emotional well-being. For instance, jaundice in infants is successfully treated with blue light because this wavelength can penetrate an infant's skin, breaking down bilirubin, making it easier to transport out of the body. Near infrared light therapy has been shown to stimulate a cellular process called ATP in human cellular biology, extending the lifespan of mitochondria, improving overall cellular function. It is well known that certain colors evoke a feeling of calmness, while others stimulate a feeling of mental alertness and even physical energy.[39] Magic practitioners use various color palettes in the construction of implements, regalia, talismans, and other tools of their trade in order to fix a portion of the corresponding force in their ritual and magical tools. Here are some color correspondences.

---

39. Ethan Waisberg, Joshua Ong, Mouayad Masalkhi, and Andrew G. Lee, "Near Infrared/Red Light Therapy a Potential Countermeasure for Mitochondrial Dysfunction in Spaceflight Associated Neuro-Ocular Syndrome (SANS)," *Eye* 38, no. 13 (2024): 2499–501, doi:10.1038/s41433-024-03091-4.

White: Kether, the Divine, light, Source, Spirit

Gray: Chokmah, the sphere of the fixed stars

Black: Binah, Saturn, the alchemical Nigredo—the dross of the first matter

Blue: Chesed, Jupiter, elemental water, philosophic essential of salt

Red: Geburah, Mars, elemental fire, the alchemical Rubedo, philosophical essential of sulfur

Yellow: Tiphareth, the sun, the alchemical Citrinas, philosophic essential of mercury

Green: Netzach, Venus, elemental earth

Orange: Hod, Mercury (planetary), also sometimes the sun

Violet: Yesod, the moon, astral plane

Citrine, Olive, Russet, Black: Malkuth, the four colors of the elemental quarters of Earth

In the ætheric magic system, which can be performed free of any specific regalia or tools, we envision a particular color in the mind's eye corresponding to the specific alchemical centers. Red corresponds to the Sulfur Center, yellow and sometimes gold correspond to the Mercury Center, and blue corresponds to the Salt Center.

Again, all things participate in a spectrum of frequency and energy. For someone familiar with music, a particular tone and color correspond to specific "notes" within a particular scale. Once the scale has been "activated" by the harmonious implementation of ritual accoutrements, the practitioner is able to access this scale (e.g., corresponding to the key of Mars, associated with the color red, elemental fire, and sulfur) and stimulate and direct its forces toward an intended effect. These scales are our universal hierarchies or chains of flow.

TEMPERATURE

Temperature is another manifestation of the energetic spectrum that exists within the greater macrocosmic ætheric field. This is known as heat energy. Temperature indicates either the presence or the absence of heat energy, which on a molecular level indicates rapidity and motion. The Empedoclean elements are based on different combinations of heat or cold and dryness or moisture.

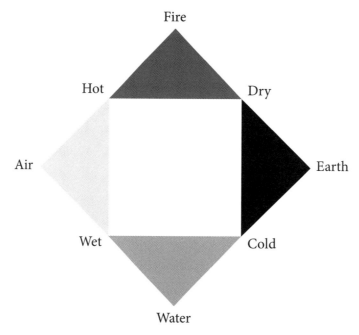

Elemental Qualities Diagram

The temperatures included in the various elemental qualities (fire—hot, air—luke-warm, water—cool, earth—cold) can be associated to the various planets and zodiacal signs by way of their elemental correspondences. I've listed the elemental correspondences of the planets in chapter 5. The twelve zodiacal signs are elementally classified by *triplicity*—the grouping of zodiacal signs into four groups of three based on the elements.

Triplicity Diagram

The Tria Prima, which will be most apropos to the ætheric magic system, also has elemental correspondences. Warmth is associated with the Sulfur Center; neutral temperature is associated with the Mercury Center; a cool temperature is associated with the Salt Center.

EXERCISE: A SYMPHONY OF SIGNATURES

Let's combine all three of our physical forces into the symphony of signatures—a harmony of sound, color, and temperature in your sphere of sensation. This exercise will allow you to develop over time the skill of being able to visualize, vibrate, and feel simultaneously and with vivid focus. With repeated practice over several months, this exercise alone will make you a magical powerhouse.

Directions

1. Assume Middle Pillar Posture and take a few deep breaths.

2. Visualize your Sulfur Center, in the center of your cranial cavity, stimulating to activity.

3. Vibrate the sound *shhh* and picture it glowing a bright, primary red.

4. Continue to vibrate the sound *shhh* while visualizing the Sulfur Center glowing red, and begin to see your entire sphere of sensation as glowing the same color red.

5. Continue vibrating the sound *shhh*, and when your sphere of sensation is radiating the color red, begin to feel the sensation of warmth all around you.

6. Continue this vibration, visualization, and feeling of the sensation of warmth until you are able to clearly sense all three aspects happening at the same time.

7. Allow these visualizations and sensations to fade and begin to visualize your Mercury Center, in the center of your chest cavity, stimulating to activity.

8. Envision it glowing bright yellow and vibrate the sound *ahhh*. The vibration should be the same pitch that causes your chest cavity to vibrate, as in the second (Middle Pillar) variation of the exercise Sounding the Centers (see page 118).

9. Continue vibrating the sound *ahhh* and see your entire sphere of sensation radiating the same color yellow.

10. At this point, the temperature you should feel is neutral or room temperature.

11. When this is firmly established, allow all images and sensations to fade.

12. Visualize your Salt Center, in your lower abdominal cavity, beginning to stimulate to activity.

13. Envision the center glowing a primary blue color and vibrate the sound *mmmm* at a low pitch.

14. Continue visualizing the center glowing blue and vibrating the sound *mmmm* and see your sphere of sensation radiating the same color blue.

15. As your sphere of sensation is radiating blue, while vibrating the sound *mmmm*, begin to feel the sensation of coolness all around you.

16. When you have established this, allow the visualizations and sensation to fade away and take a few deep, centering breaths.

17. Close out and come back to the room you are in.

18. Record any thoughts, emotions, or insights in your journal.

CONCLUSION

Magic can be simple—not necessarily easy, but simple. The utilization of physical forces such as sound, color, and temperature are keystones of magical practice throughout its long history. You'll find the use of particular colors in garb, implements, and other ritual accoutrement, as well as the vibration of words, names, and sounds. Likewise, the use of the elements is indicative of their various qualities, including temperature, as a central feature in much of magic. In the ætheric magic system, you can utilize all these forces in order to fully express, isolate, and project a particular essence, quality, or force, imbuing your sphere of sensation with these and making them available for use in any kind of magic.

CHAPTER 8
PRELIMINARY TECHNIQUES
OF ÆTHERIC MAGIC

In the course of your journey through this book, you have learned about the history and theory of ætheric magic by a comparative examination of ancient techniques and systems of energy work and magic. You have also engaged in a thorough amount of exercises, which are meant to attune you to your own ætheric field and begin cultivating and moving ætheric energy inside your sphere of sensation. The next step is to begin applying your acquired mastery over your ætheric field to the postures and techniques of magic.

I will now begin to focus on several magical techniques that constitute the foundations of ritual magical operations. To these I have included appended correspondences that will help us in selecting particular energies to work with by way of our universal hierarchies or chains of flow.

PRELIMINARY NOTES

There are a few important things to keep in mind during the performance of these rites. You should not rush through them. The visualizations should be clear and vivid, and you should remain relaxed both physically and mentally so that you can feel the æther moving through your body as you direct it toward and into the visualizations you have projected into your working space. The exteriorized visualizations should be empowered by the ætheric energy, carefully using the method of breath work we have established—inhale to draw in, exhale to project.

A benefit of performing the Uniting Above and Below exercise (page 92) before beginning this ritual is that you are sourcing power from the earth and stars—drawing inward the various receptive and projective energies from the ætheric field of the immediate environment. This enables the practitioner to cultivate, direct, and project ætheric energy outward without diminishing their own stores of it. When an individual becomes deficient in their own stores of ætheric energy, they may over time become weak and prone to illnesses, developing a weakened constitution to a lesser or greater degree. Therefore, you must source the energies that empower your ritual from universal or macrocosmic æther. You will undoubtedly exert some of your own microcosmic æther, but you will end up considerably less drained afterward.

The basic techniques of ritual magic are as follows:

- Projection
- Invocation
- Evocation
- Banishing, warding, exorcism
- Binding
- Consecration
- Vision work, scrying

Projection, invocation, and evocation are preliminary, or basic, techniques that we will be concentrating on in this chapter. The others will be described in the next chapter.

All the following exercises should alternately be performed both with eyes closed and with eyes open. Being able to visualize with eyes closed is a useful skill; however, as an ætheric magic practitioner, you should also try to see ætheric energy and astral forms projected by the imaginal faculty into the room around you. If you are someone who has difficulty with visualization, it may be useful to begin practicing it with eyes closed and then practicing with eyes open at a later time, once the skill has been developed.

PROJECTION

Projection is an essential technique used in most ritual work. For instance, projection is a key feature in banishing, warding, and the charging and consecration of talismans and talismanic implements. It can also be used to charge objects for ritual intake, such as a cup of wine or paten of bread or salt. One excellent use of projection is in the consecration of ætherically charged water.

The basis of projection is the movement of ætheric energy—and intention—toward a specific area or object. In order to project ætheric energy, we must first accumulate and center it. This is where our Middle Pillar and alchemical centers come under full theoretical examination. The exercise of Uniting Above and Below given in chapter 6 is foundational to the technique of projection.

In blending the energies of above (celestial/fiery) with the energies of the below (earthy) in the central anatomical center of alchemical mercury, we balance the entirety of the system and create a mediating relationship that is heart centered, having a certain malleability, and can more easily take on the qualities inherent to less-straightforward energies than the elemental. For instance, the qualities associated with the planet Jupiter or the zodiacal sign Scorpio can be projected from this center after cultivating the necessary resonance within the sphere of sensation with certain colors, sounds, and visualizations. Things like corresponding incense and talismans can also play a part but aren't essential to effectiveness. In the ætheric magic system, the combination of posture, sound, color, and visualization is entirely enough to awaken, condition, and project energy essential to a magical working.

EXERCISE: PROJECTION

The following basic exercise will give you the opportunity to work on projection.

Directions

1. Assume Middle Pillar Posture and take a few deep breaths, relaxing your body and tuning in to your sphere of sensation.

2. Imagine your Mercury Center at the center of your chest filling up with white scintillating light—ætheric energy.

3. When the sensation reaches fullness, bring your hands up along your sides, palms facing upward, arms bent at the elbows.

4. Upon reaching the level of your Mercury Center, thrust your arms forward as if pushing something away from your chest while stepping forward with the right leg.

5. As you push forward with your arms, make sure to turn your arms inward so that your palms end facing downward, toward the ground, when your arms reach full extension in front of you.

6. Center your vision directly between your hands. This is the basic technique of projection.

Projecting from the Center

The Mercury Center is typically used for projection of forces for charging, consecration, and healing others. When at a distance, we project a healing force from our Mercury/Tiphareth Center, and when healing hands-on, we activate the Mercury/Tiphareth Center and direct its energies by way of the Projection and Reception Points in the hands. It can also be utilized in magical evocation and invocation. Mercury posture is used to awaken and balance ætheric energy and charge the energetic body in preparation for ritual or energy work. The Salt Center is best for the accumulation and rooting of energies, as well as storing ætheric energy for one's own health and longevity.

It is also our magical battery—a storage container for personal ætheric force made available for use in ritual and magical works. The Salt Center also stimulates the creative energies of Yesod, which, as mentioned earlier, are psycho-sexual in nature. This is a powerful center for manifestation magic. However, there is a potential danger for sexual overwhelm when energy is projected from this center. Therefore, we always sublimate this energy, by raising it to the Mercury/Tiphareth Center before projection. All this said, let's take a look at the movement, breath work, and visualization that should accompany projection.

Basic Movements for Projections

The basic movement for projection posture is a raising of the arms and hands from about hip level to about eye level on inhalation, then thrusting forward the arms, palms open, facing downward with fingers closed, but relaxed on the exhalation. This is done directly toward the direction an image is being projected or energy is being moved into an object. The practitioner should focus their sight intently and directly between their hands, which is where the direction or object should be located. At the moment of projection, along with the hands being thrown forward and the eyes focused between them at the object to which we are projecting ætheric energy, the right foot of the practitioner should step forward about six inches and step back when the projection is finished.

Projection Posture, Step 1

Projection Posture, Step 2

Projection Posture, Step 3

The direction of the flow of energy in the projection technique should be first inward (toward the sphere of sensation, either up from the earth in the case of earth energies or downward in the case of spiritual, fiery, planetary, or zodiacal energies) and through the Middle Pillar. In the case we are pulling energy up through the Malkuth-Yesod axis of the Salt Center, it should come upward through the Middle Pillar to the Mercury Center before being projected out of the Mercury Center utilizing the projection technique. In the case of, say, the invocation of planetary or zodiacal energies to the end of charging, and consecrating a talisman, it would come in through the Kether-Da'ath axis of the Sulfur Center, pass through the Middle Pillar to the Salt Center, and then move back upward to the Mercury Center to be projected. This ensures that the energy receives grounding in the manifestation center and is imparted with the sexual energies necessary to creation.

The breathing for this should be an inhalation to take energy in and raise it to the necessary centers, followed by a powerful exhalation when it is projected. The practitioner should have the sensation of filling themselves up with the particular energy and the projection should last until the practitioner feels that this force has been "emptied." The visualization of all this intake and movement of energy should be in the form of a beam of bright white light. Visualize the beam of light ceasing, having left your body, and imagine the image or talismanic object as glowing with a charge. We will utilize our ætheric vision to test this in a later technique.

EXERCISE: ACTIVATING THE SPHERES

Specific centers can be further activated before drawing intended energy inward by the use of the respective postures, vibratory sounds, and associated color visualizations. In the following exercise, you will powerfully activate the Mercury Center. The same methods are used to stimulate the Salt Center, with its appropriate location, sound, and color. However, if energy itself, such as a planetary, elemental, or healing energy, is to be projected toward something, it should be visualized as a beam or ray of light exiting the Middle Pillar through the Mercury Center.

If an *image* is to be projected, as in the case of our warding rite, then the image should be formulated in the triangular space between the hands in Sulfur Posture and projected from there. This has to do with the imaginal faculty of the eye of the mind—the third eye. If that image is to be charged with a certain force, then this should be followed by the visualization of the projected force as a beam coming from the Mercury Center, having utilized this Middle Pillar formula of invocation and projection. The energy we desire to be projected can be built up and concentrated in various centers with the assistance of vibration. If, say, the energies of elemental earth need to be concentrated, you can visualize the corresponding center (Malkuth Center) as being filled with its energy, glowing brighter and more voluminous with each vibration of the elementally associated name (Ge, Terra, Gaia, Geb, etc.).

Directions

1. First establish the Middle Pillar by imagining your Spirit Crown and Earth Grounding Points open and receiving ætheric energy from the above and below—the celestial and the terrestrial.

2. Then utilize the in-breath to center this energy in the Mercury Center, seeing it accumulated there.

3. Next, assume Mercury Posture or Quintessence Posture and vibrate the mother sound corresponding to mercury and the Hebrew mother letter of air, Aleph—*ahhh*.

4. Envision the center radiating a bright yellow-gold color, which infuses your entire sphere of sensation. To move this energy, it must be projected.

Stop Posture

Sealing

In traditional magical lineages, there is an idea that projected energy called "force" or "current" could rebound back on the projector. To block this rebound, sealing it into whatever or wherever it has been projected, the Sign of Silence was used in some traditions. This posture is a placing of the index finger over the closed lips and stomping of the foot, as if giving a sign to be silent. This can be utilized if preferable; otherwise, the ætheric magic practitioner will stomp the left foot while dropping the left arm to the side, leaving the right arm and hand extended in a posture signaling *stop*.

INVOCATION

Invocation utilizes the hierarchies or chains of flow in order to activate, extract, and draw down a particular type of energy into your sphere of sensation using the vibration of words and names, as well as visualization and breath work. You can use any system of correspondent intelligences, such as the Pseudo-Dionysian and Agrippan hierarchies. These hierarchies refer to the hierarchies of intelligences codified by the Christian Neoplatonist Pseudo-Dionysius the Areopagite, which were adopted by Heinrich Cornelius Agrippa in his *Three Books of Occult Philosophy*. See appendix B for more details. But just for a quick example, as your invocatory chain of flow, be sure to invoke the highest first and work your way down in hierarchical order. Any invocatory method can be used, including the hexagram rituals of the Golden Dawn and the heptagram invocation of the Ordo Aurum Solis.

The basic posture of invocation is having the elbows bent at about 45 degrees, palms facing upward and spread apart to just outside of the shoulder on either side. Eyes should be inclined upward about 45 degrees.

The attendant energy being called forth during the invocation of an energy should be visualized as coming downward as a beam of light if it is planetary, zodiacal, angelic, or of the active elements air and fire. It can be visualized as coming upward from the earth if it is of the receptive elements earth and water. If you are drawing energy down from above, the energy should pass through the Salt Center by way of the Middle Pillar and move down to the Malkuth Center at the feet and ground, before being moved back up to the Mercury Center. This movement of the light should be visualized steadily and not too fast to avoid potential disorientation or nausea. This energy should also be seen as infusing the entirety of the sphere of sensation.

Invocation Posture

EXERCISE: INVOCATION

A really powerful way to perform an invocation is to recite your invocatory poem or sentences over your altar facing the elemental quarter or actual physical direction of the planet or zodiacal constellation you are drawing power from. The sidereal location of the constellations and planets can be obtained using any variety of good, reliable apps.

Directions

1. Assume Middle Pillar Posture.

2. When you are ready to draw the energy into your sphere of sensation, move toward the elemental quarter, planetary body, or constellation you are drawing power from and turn your back to it, thus becoming the hierophant of the element, planet, or zodiacal sign.

3. Recite an invocatory passage such as one among the classic text of Hellenic invocatory magic, the hymns of Orpheus.

4. Pull down the light, visualizing it in the corresponding color of the element, planet, or zodiacal sign, while vibrating the names of the chain of flow.

5. See and feel the energy completely filling and charging the Middle Pillar, being infused throughout the entire sphere of sensation.

6. From here, any variety of uses can be made of the energy once powerfully invoked in this manner, such as charging and consecrating a talisman, projecting an image, sending this energy somewhere or to someone, or generally infusing the sphere of sensation with it for use throughout the day or in another working.

This energy can also be "locked" into the sphere of sensation for a prescribed period of time by visualizing the associated symbol or related sigil that expresses the energy inside a fire triangle over the Sulfur Center and can be projected or released at a later time.

EVOCATION

Whereas our previous invocation utilized specific energies to be infused or projected, evocation typically involves the calling forth of the intelligence(s) of a particular energy or ætheric chain of flow. This typically involves visualization of varying kinds. The method of evocation I'll be giving you uses the visualization and projection of a telematic image, which is then charged and consecrated. When calling on disembodied intelligences that express a particular individuation of a part of the ætheric scale or chain (such as an archangel, for instance), the safest and most effective way to proceed is to create an image through which the intelligence can express itself.

However, in order to be sure that we actually get what we're calling for, the image we craft should be harmonious with the aspects the archangel (or any other entity) embodies. For instance, the archangel Michael might be wearing green robes beneath red armor. Michael may wield a fiery sword or have a fiery countenance—flame-red eyes and wild, bright red hair. Beyond this cursory recommendation, I leave the astral images to be used in evocation to the ingenium of the practitioner.

EXERCISE: EVOCATION

The following exercise will get you started. In the case of any force or forces to be evoked, except those of a qlipphotic or demonic nature, we will first follow our formula of evocation. I do not recommend pulling in energy that is qlipphotic, because these forces, by definition, are imbalanced, and the practitioner of ætheric magic should strive to achieve and maintain balance. When we draw in and bring to the fore one specific force, such as, say, the force of fire and Mars (corresponding to microcosmic Geburah), it has a natural affinity to its counterbalance (Chesed on our microcosmic Tree of Life) in our own sphere of sensation, which is still a part of the mix though not taking center stage. None of these forces is inherently imbalanced the way qlipphotic forces are.

Directions

1. Assume Middle Pillar Posture.
2. When you are ready to evoke, stand across your altar from the quarter or other location where the power you wish to call forth is represented either elementally or celestially.
3. Begin your verbal evocation, utilizing your preferred system of hierarchies or calls.
4. Your sphere of sensation should begin to become infused with the appropriate energy or force
5. When you feel filled with it, the astral image you have selected or created in your mind's eye is formed and projected via the Sulfur Posture method of projection.
6. Next, the energy should be moved through the Middle Pillar in the usual fashion: through the Salt Center (lower abdominal cavity) on an inhalation and back up to the Mercury Center (center of chest cavity).

7. When the energy is centered in your Mercury Center, forcefully project from the Mercury Center on an exhalation.

8. The last step is to perform a recitation of the verbal evocation and to vibrate the names of power sequentially down through the hierarchical chain. These calls should be repeated with force and in an authoritative tone of voice until the astral image that has been prepared and charged begins to come alive with its own sentience. This astral image is also called a *telesmatic* image in that it serves as an astral-ætheric talisman for any invoked energy, spirit, or intelligence.

Notes

If this is your first time performing such an evocation, I should make a note that serious evocation can typically require certain periods of preparation, such as fasting, prayer, and meditation. Also, it can be startling when an image comes alive—remember to remain focused. If need be, you can always shut the operation down by a quick banishing, but remain in control of the situation.

Inflaming the Sphere of Sensation

There is another component of the techniques of invocation and evocation that is not as easily spoken of. It has to be felt by the practitioner and typically requires a little practice. When calling forth particular entities and ætheric chains, *the call is key*. There should be present a degree of what might be called, for lack of a better term, heart fire. This relates particularly to the magical faculty of the will. In attempting to explain this, I defer to the classical magical axiom "Inflame thyself with prayer."

In the course of developing your ætheric perceptual senses and cultivating and moving your ætheric energy, you may notice certain sensations that accompany particular exercises, namely the drawing in of spirit, light, power—ætheric energy by any other name. This sensation can be overwhelming, but you can get ahold of it by utilizing deep, controlled, rhythmic breathing and gently moving it around your broader sphere of sensation in order to diffuse it throughout your ætheric field. I call this sensation a power surge, because that's exactly what it feels like. It feels like I'm being pumped full of energy. My hair stands on end and I get goose bumps, my breathing become deep and strong; my arms and hands begin to buzz with the feeling of ætheric energy, along with other important energy points on my body, swirling into greater activity. Most significant, however, is that my consciousness becomes extraordinarily vivid. Colors, scents, and even the sensation of the air can become almost overwhelmingly vivid and stark. It is at this point that magic has its greatest potential for efficacy, as the sphere of sensation is completely infused with an influx of ætheric energy, which can—and should—be readily directed toward your ritual objective, whether that be manifesting an intention, the consecration of a talisman, or some other end.

Independent of any formal ritual involving the visualization of the drawing down of ætheric energy, invocatory prayer itself is an extraordinary technique for accomplishing this power surge of energy. Selecting a prayer or hymn that touches you at a deep level is important, but the reading (preferably memorization, but reading is also fine) of this prayer or hymn in a committed way—a confident, powerful, and emotionally charged reading—is essential to the cultivation of this power and its associated sensation.

CONCLUSION

Invocation, evocation, and projection are primary techniques in magic generally and will be built upon and utilized in the expanded techniques for ritual, which I will give you in the next chapter. It is my hope that you are beginning to understand at a deeper level how all the pieces—ætheric energy, focus, intention, visualization, words, and cultivation of interior states—contribute to the synthesis of forces that magic fundamentally is. Be sure that you have gone through each of the exercises given in this chapter before moving to the next.

CHAPTER 9
EXPANDED TECHNIQUES

Having covered the basic preliminary techniques of magic, I'll now begin to walk you through several expanded techniques, including banishing, warding, and exorcism; binding; and consecration. Throughout the course of working these techniques, you'll incorporate the basics you have already learned in the previous chapters. The first major technique to be mastered in effective magical training is typically banishing, and so I'll begin with this technique, expanding as we go along.

THE INVOKING AND BANISHING PENTAGRAM

While the technique of drawing an invoking pentagram is cursorily mentioned in other parts of this chapter, I include it here as an exercise for those of you who may not be entirely familiar with it. As an essential technique for much of Western ceremonial magic after the late nineteenth century, it's important to be familiar with it. The Ritual of the Pentagram, which elaborates the elemental scheme of the pentagram itself, was created by the founders of the Hermetic Order of the Golden Dawn, a magical society that emerged in London, England, in the 1880s.

The pentagram exemplifies five angles or points that are all tied together in a unicursal (single line) geometry, making it a perfect symbol for our five-element system delineated in chapters 5 and 6. The quaternary elements (fire, air, water, earth) are conceived as coexisting inseparably with one another and within the quintessence, or fifth element, of æther. The pentagram is a visual depiction of this integral relationship. At each of its angles is attributed a particular element, with spirit (æther, in our system) at the apex of the figure to represent its primacy and governance over the quaternary elements. At the right arm of the pentagram is the element of water; at the right leg the element of fire; at the left leg the element of earth; at the left arm the element of air.

Pentagram

EXERCISE: DRAWING AN INVOKING AND BANISHING PENTAGRAM

Directions: Banishing Pentagram

1. Standing straight, begin with your arm and fingers extended, pointing at an angle near your lower left foot, and move your arm and hand in a single stroke from there toward the apex of the pentagram, just over your head; complete the rest of the pentagram unicursally—with fluid movement.

2. The order of elemental angles is as follows: Begin at the lower left, moving to the apex of the pentagram (earth angle to spirit angle), then moving from the

apex to the angle of fire at the lower right; move from lower right to the angle of air at the upper left (just outside your left shoulder); then move across horizontally from upper left to the angle of water at the upper right (just outside of your right shoulder), and upper right to lower left back to the angle of earth, where we began.

Directions: Invoking Pentagram

1. Begin with your arm and finger extended at the apex (spirit angle) of the pentagram, at arm's length just above your head.

2. Move your extended arm and hand downward to the bottom left (earth) and proceed to complete the pentagram moving in that direction of flow.

Invoking Earth   Invoking Fire

Invoking Water   Invoking Air

Banishing Earth   Banishing Fire

Banishing Water   Banishing Air

Invoking and Banishing Pentagram Table

BANISHING

Banishing is used as a ritual preliminary to delineate the boundaries of and clear a space for working, essentially creating a kind of magical vessel or container. It marks a liminal space, where the old is being cleared away for the new—a process of dissolution toward a state of potentiality.

In ætheric magic, corresponding centers and postures are utilized along with breath work and visualization to ritually perform a banishing. We will now also begin incorporating the vibration of divine names and words of power, as well as the projection of visualizations outside of the mind and sphere of sensation. Banishing is typically composed of some degree of projection and involves the casting of a circle and protective wards, as well as the evocation of archangelic forces. Uses of banishing are generally to clear a particular space for a working and cleanse it of any unwanted astral-ætheric influences. Good times to use a banishing are before a divination of some kind, before a meditation or vision work session, and before a magical working.

We will cover some basic rituals that may be familiar to the practitioner of Western ceremonial magic and that may be new to some. You will precede the banishing with a brief performance of the Uniting Above and Below exercise on page 92.

EXERCISE: QABALISTIC CROSS

The Qabalistic Cross is a brief preliminary rite that serves to equilibrate the sphere of sensation before a working. You will typically find it appended to many rituals of ceremonial magic that came out of the Hermetic Order of the Golden Dawn and its various offshoot organizations in the late nineteenth and early twentieth centuries, since this is where it originates as a discrete rite, usually paired with the Ritual of the Pentagram, which the founder of the Golden Dawn created.

Being Qabalistic, the technique utilizes the framework of the Tree of Life in the sphere of sensation and serves to create a vertical, or Y, axis by uniting the sphere of Kether (crown) with the sphere of Malkuth (kingdom) and a horizontal, or X, axis by uniting the sphere of Chesed (mercy) with the sphere of Geburah (severity). It also establishes a connection with Highest Divinity by invoking the transcendent light into the sphere of sensation by way of the Kether Center (crown of the head). This vertical axis establishes a Pillar of Spirit in the center of our circle at the outset, around which we will build our ritual circle.

This short rite is powerful and serves as a total equilibration and ætheric charging of the sphere of sensation of the practitioner.

Directions

1. Stand in the center of your ritual space facing east. If you have an altar (strongly recommended), stand west of the altar, facing east.

2. Take a few deep, centering breaths and be sure to relax any bodily, mental, or emotional tension. When this is achieved, in your mind's eye, picture the infinite expanse of the Ain Soph Aur vast and far above you, beyond the abyss.

3. Reach up with your right hand (open palm) and draw light from this source down to form a sphere of bright, scintillating white light just above you, the sphere sitting atop your head like a crown. This is your Kether Center. Touch the point of your third eye in the center of your forehead just above the eyes with the middle finger of your open hand. As the drawing down of the light is being done, vibrate *Atah* ("thou art/you are").

Qabalistic Cross 1

4. Maintain the connection with Highest Divinity and draw the light downward in a straight line with your open hand to a point just below the navel on the midline of your body.

5. Touch here and vibrate *Malkuth* ("the kingdom").

Qabalistic Cross 2

6. See the shaft of light descend to and end here, but see also another sphere of scintillating white light form at your feet. The top half of the sphere encompasses your feet. The bottom half reaches into the ground below them. This is your Malkuth Center. Again, to reiterate, the movement of your open hand and the shaft of light stop at the point below the navel. We are attempting to establish an equal-armed cross, not a Christian cross, in the sphere of sensation. To that end, you should picture the shafts of light created by this ritual as running through your body, not overlain onto it.

7. Reach up with your open right hand and touch your right shoulder. Vibrate *Ve Geburah* ("and the power"). See a sphere of white scintillating light form just outside your right shoulder. This is your Geburah Center.

Qabalistic Cross 3

8. Draw the shaft of light from this sphere across your chest and touch the left shoulder, seeing another scintillating white light sphere forming just outside your left shoulder as you vibrate *Ve Gedulah* ("and the glory"). This is your Chesed Center.

Qabalistic Cross 4

9. Reach both arms out to stand in the form of a cross while vibrating *Le Olam* ("unto the ages"). Feel strongly the two intersecting shafts of light established through you.

Qabalistic Cross 5/Tau Posture

10. Bring your hands together at the point where the shafts intersect at the center of your chest and vibrate *Amen*. See another sphere of pure, scintillating white light form at your Tiphareth Center.

11. Take a moment to observe any thoughts or feelings that arise after the completion of this ritual and to place yourself firmly back in the actual physical space you are in before opening your eyes if they have been closed for its performance.

EXERCISE: THE CALYX

As an alternative to the Qabalistic Cross for practitioners more aligned to Greek-pagan magic, you may use a rite that accomplishes the same purpose from the pagan tradition of the Ordo Aurum Solis, called the *Calyx*, meaning "chalice." Again, with this rite, you are invoking, receiving, and equilibrating ætheric energy in its purest spiritual form as preparation for ritual work and establishing the Pillar of Spirit in the center of your circle.

Calyx

Directions

1. Stand in the center of your ritual space facing east. If you have an altar (strongly recommended), stand west of the altar, facing east.

2. Visualize a flame just above your head with your hands raised shoulder height in a cross or Tau position. Vibrate *Ei* (*ay-ee*, "you are").

3. Inhale and visualize a beam of light from this flame descending to a sphere at your feet. Then exhale and vibrate '*H Basilea* (*hee vah-see-LAY-ah*, "the Kingdom").

4. Inhale and bring the left hand to the right shoulder. Exhale and vibrate *Kai 'H Dynamis* (*kay hee thee-NAH-meez*, "and the power").

5. Inhale and bring the right hand to the left shoulder, crossing the arms over the chest. Exhale and vibrate *Kai 'H Doxa* (*kay hee DOKE-sah*, "and the glory").

6. Inhale while raising your head to look upward. Feel the beam of light strongly within your Middle Pillar. Exhale and vibrate *Eis Tous Aionas* (*ay-eez toos eye-OH-nas*, "unto the ages").

7. Take a moment to observe any thoughts and feelings that arise after the completion of this ritual, and to place yourself firmly back in the actual physical space you are in before opening your eyes if they have been closed for its performance.

EXERCISE: SETTING THE GATES—A WARDING RITE

In this banishing/warding rite, I will include alternate Hebrew and Greek divine names and visualizations to give alternatives for the practitioner's preference. Again, these can be substituted for other languages and pantheons as the practitioner sees fit. Feel free to substitute a Wiccan circle-casting ritual here for instance.

Directions

1. After completing the brief preliminary rite (the Qabalistic Cross, the Calyx, or another rite if you prefer), assume Middle Pillar Posture in the center of your space facing east (or west of your altar facing east, as the case may be).

2. Come around to stand in the east of your working space, facing the east. Bring your hands to Salt Posture, and on an inhalation, visualize the light of the ætheric energy rising from the cauldron of the Salt Center up the Middle Pillar to your Sulfur Center. As this happens, raise your arms and hands to follow the light, while keeping the hands in posture, going from Salt Posture to Quintessence Posture, ending in Sulfur Posture in as fluid a motion as possible.

3. Vibrate the sound *shhh*. Visualize your Sulfur Center as growing warm, diffusing your body with the color red, and from there radiating outward to your sphere of sensation.

4. When this is achieved, visualize a pentagram of bright white light in the triangle made by your hands in front of your Sulfur Center.

5. When the pentagram is fully visualized, throw both hands forward into the Projection Sign, and see the pentagram projected to the eastern quarter of your working space just outside your intended circle, as if casting it forth. The distance it is cast will vary depending on the size of your space and intended circle. Its proportions should be about equal with your own; the uppermost point should be slightly higher than your own head, the points of the arms should extend slightly beyond the width of your shoulders, and the lowermost two points should extend to just outside either of your hips. This "casting" is done rather than "tracing" or drawing the pentagram in front of us.

6. Drop the reception hand to your side, holding the projection hand palm downward, fingers extended toward the center of the pentagram. The practitioner can vibrate either the Hebrew divine name YHVH (*yode-hay-vahv-hay*) or the Greek *Athanatos* (*ah-thah-NAH-toze*). The practitioner can also feel free to substitute appropriate divine names of any pantheon of their choosing.

7. Projection hand extended, turn or walk to the south, visualizing your hand tracing a curved line of bright-white light from the pentagram in the east to the southern quarter of your working space.

8. Bring your hands up the Middle Pillar once more, in a fluid motion, ending in Sulfur Posture. Visualize a pentagram in the space of the triangle between your hands, and cast it forth again with the projection sign.

9. Same as before, drop the reception hand, and keep the projection hand raised and centered on the pentagram in the south. Vibrate *Adonai* (*AH-doe-nye*) or *Kyrios* (*kee-REE-ohs*) and visualize the pentagram as strongly charged.

10. Repeat this in the west, vibrating *Eheieh* (*eh-HAY-yeh*) or *Pancrates* (*pahn-CRAH-taze*).

11. Repeat in the north, vibrating *AGLA* (*AH-gah-lah*) or *Theos* (*THAY-ohs*).

12. Complete the circle by bringing the projection hand back to the center of the pentagram in the east. Then return to the center of the space or west of the altar facing east and assume Tau Posture (legs and feet together, arms extended straight out to the sides, head lightly tilted back).

13. Visualize a large pillar of bright white light in the east behind the pentagram, rising from the floor to at least the height of the ceiling. Say, "Before me," and vibrate (intone) *Raphael*, or say, "To the east," and vibrate *Soter*.

14. Remain facing east and, visualizing another Pillar of Light in the west, say, "Behind me," and vibrate *Gabriel*. Alternately, say, "To the west," then vibrate *Asphaleus*.

15. Visualize another pillar in the south, saying, "At my right hand," then vibrate *Michael*. Alternately, say, "To the South," then vibrate *Alastor*.

16. Visualize another pillar in the north, saying, "At my left hand," and vibrate *Uriel*. Alternately, "To the north," and vibrate *Amyntor*.

17. Visualize a column of very bright white light running vertically though the center of your circle. Then say, "Around me flames the fiery pentagram, and in midst of all shines the Column of Spirit."

18. You can end this exercise with a Qabalistic Cross, the Calyx, Uniting Above and Below (see page 92), or a combination of these.

ASTRAL-ÆTHERIC GATEWAYS

In setting wards to the four quarters of the working container of your magical circle, you have not placed gates that merely guard, but also those from which you can pull in specific types of ætheric energy. The doorway through which these energies enter your space is a pentagon formed at the center of each pentagram. The purpose of a warding rite such as this is to create a sterile field, so to speak, clearing the elemental permutations of ætheric energy from a space, which are typically present in a mixed and imbalanced form.

To summon or draw in the particular energies of elemental air, use the pentagon in the east; for fire, the south; for water, the west; and for earth, the north; such as in, say, consecrating a talismanic implement to one of the elements. Be sure that you are envisioning a column of spirit that is at the center of your circle (established by the preliminary rite of invocation—either the Qabalistic Cross or Calyx) and is firmly established before calling in any elemental energies or entities. Again, we can think of these energies as intelligent because they are. They can communicate with and obey the requests and commands of our minds. To do this, they often appear to us in a cognizable form dependent on our own personal available imagery—the images in the contents of our imagination.

Finally, a word about the archangelic presences called in to the four quarters. You may, if you prefer, visualize the images of the archangels or gods of a particular pantheon in these quarters. However, I have retained the visualization prescribed by the earliest iteration of the Lesser Ritual of the Pentagram, a warding rite created by the founders of the Hermetic Order of the Golden Dawn in 1880s London. Over time, these pillars of light associated with the archangelic presences morphed into their anthropomorphized images, along with elemental colors attributed to their robes. However, I find it important to keep in mind that the archangelic stations are not necessarily the archangels themselves—they are astral-ætheric wards created by us, through which a portion of their essence or power is present with us in our ritual. It is not a full-on evocation of an archangelic being. The same is true when using deity-form visualizations in the quarters. You may add any further protocols you prefer in addition to this warding rite, such as censing and asperging, for example.

EXORCISM

It is necessary in the case of, say, charging and consecrating a talisman or other such item that the material basis first be exorcised or banished of any residual or unspecified energies. This is a further step in our creation of a sterile field within our magical container or vessel for working. This can be done simply by drawing a banishing earth pentagram over the material and uttering certain banishing commands and incantations recited in a powerful voice and strongly reinforced by the will.

When exorcising a particular physical object, you are banishing all unwanted influences from it. To some extent, all materials possess some form of energy that builds up over time like a static charge. To train your focus on the particular item and address the intelligent energies that are residing in its material basis, you should designate the particular item elementally. For example, if you are purging water for the consecration of ætherically charged ritual water, you should address the item being exorcised as "Creature of Water." If it is a piece of metal for a talisman, address it as "Creature of Earth." For incense I would recommend "Creature of Air," and any kind of light or torch, "Creature of Fire." Here is a sample exhortation for the exorcism of water.

EXERCISE: AN EXORCISM OF WATER

You will want to achieve a state of alert relaxation for this basic technique. What we are attempting to do here is cultivate a state of elemental spirit in the ætheric field of the substance we are intending to use for some ritual (or other) purpose—in this case, water. We do this by banishing any unwanted elemental expressions of the water's ætheric field that are imbalanced, rendering the water's ætheric field as a pure state of unconditioned æther.

When you have gathered an appropriate amount of water for your purposes (say, eight to ten ounces for a container of ritual purificatory water), pour it into a bowl or basin and set it on your altar. Keep the container you intend to keep the water in after the exorcism nearby. You may need a funnel to get the water from the basin or bowl into its primary container. While this exercise focuses on the exorcism of a substance, there is typically a second part to this that involves the ritual consecration (empowering and dedication) of the water toward some spiritual purpose.

Directions

1. Assume Middle Pillar Posture and take a few deep breaths, until you are centered and focused.

2. Perform the Qabalistic Cross.

3. Begin the exorcism by holding your hand of projection, palm downward, about three to six inches directly above the surface of the water.

4. Direct your attention as acutely as possible to the water. Look directly at the water for the duration of the working.

5. In a commanding voice, say, "Creature of Water! I hereby command that you be exorcized of all impure and unwanted influences, that you may be made a fitting substance for (state intended use for the water). In the name of (state preferred deity, angel, archangel, or any other intelligence you have chosen to represent the power of formidable banishment), I command that you be cleansed (+), purified (+), and banished (+) of all unwanted influences." At each of the + symbols, you will make an equal armed cross over the surface of the water, starting with the vertical line from top to bottom, then the horizontal line moving from left to right.

6. Try to use some of your developed ætheric senses to see what color the ætheric field of the water is and how far it is visible from its surface. Take note of

any tactile sensations in the palm of your hand as it hovers over the water. This may tell you something about the efficacy of the exorcism at this point.

7. Repeat the above exhortation as many times as necessary before you feel the water is free of any unwanted energies. Use your intuition to gauge when this is accomplished.

8. When you feel the water is cleansed, perform a closing out and another equilibrating rite (Qabalistic Cross or Calyx, for instance).

9. At this point, you may pour it carefully into its primary container.

BINDING

For magical evocation that involves entities of a specifically chaotic or potentially problematic nature, particularly entities of the goetic and Solomonic traditions of magic or entities with whom pacts will be made generally, binding is essential. In goetic (from the Greek *goes*, meaning "sorcerer") and Solomonic traditions (named after the biblical King Solomon) of magic, entities—typically ranging from the demonic to the angelic and everything in between—are summoned for the purposes of acquiring particular goals, items, or knowledge, sometimes using coercive methods on the part of the sorcerer or ceremonial magician. This type of magic is typically referred to as *conjuration*. Contact made with these entities is referred to as "gateway images" by David Rankine in his *Grimoire Encyclopaedia* and is described in the same work as a "form by which a spiritual creature is perceived, acting as an agreed interface between the spirit and the conjuror."[40]

A Triangle of Art in the system of ætheric magic should be made of an electrolytic substance, such as physical salt, then charged by the practitioner with their Projection Point hand, slowly and carefully tracing the salt outline, while visualizing and feeling the ætheric charge flowing from the center of the palm or pads of the fingers. When tracing, be sure not to cut corners—literally. Make sure the figure is closed at the corners, in tracing and in visualization. This projection of energy from the hand is essentially the Consecration Posture or technique. The Triangle of Art should be visualized as glowing when charged. *All gateway images should be projected into the Triangle of Art, and the triangle should never be broken.*

The posture most relevant to the operation of binding is the same as described in the tracing of the magical circle in the warding rite given above.

---

40. David Rankine, *The Grimoire Encyclopaedia*, vol. 1 (West Yorkshire, UK: Hadean Press, 2023), 26.

EXERCISE: BINDING

1. Assume Middle Pillar Posture.

2. Be sure the entity evoked is within the Triangle of Art.

3. Stand up straight with your left arm at rest at your side and your right arm extended. Your hand should be extended flat, with all fingers pointing forward and palm downward. Remember to remain relaxed in your posture, joints, and fingers—avoid being too rigid.

4. Fix your gaze at the entity evoked.

5. Visualize your arm and hand as a spear or sword. This is the Command Posture. The Command Posture may also be used when reciting banishing incantations over the material basis of a talisman as mentioned earlier.

Command Posture

6. See the evoked entity bound about with a bright white rope of ætheric energy. Be sure that this rope is not attached to any part of your body, regalia, or anything else outside the Triangle of Art. Do not release the entity from this bondage and do not lower your arm—keep your fingers straight and pointed like the tip of a sharp implement at the entity.

7. Perform whatever task or contract the entity has been evoked for, remaining in the Command Posture.

8. When finished, recite a *license to depart*, giving the entity freedom to leave and return immediately to its natural habitation.

9. Perform a banishing and end the working.

10. Record your experiences and insights in your journal.

This technique should only be used with spirits of a lesser degree of potential danger, and the visualization of the arm and hand as a weapon of war is paramount. In traditional Goetic and Solomonic conjuration, the letter of the ritual should be followed. I advise you make no substitutions in this respect. Therefore, if it calls for a sword, use a sword. Imagine ætheric energy flowing into it, binding it to your hand, making it an extension of your body. It is also advisable that the hierarchical chain of flow be invoked before any lesser spirit, intelligence, or being is called forth—invoke the highest *first*!

CONSECRATION

Consecration is the magical act of empowering a substance or item with a particular type of ætheric energy. This could be a statue, a talisman, purificatory water, ritual candles—even your ritual wardrobe! At the point of consecration, which typically follows exorcizing or banishing the material of unwanted influence, the substance or item is committed to that specific chain of ætheric force. This means, for instance, that if the item is consecrated to the planet Mars, it will have an affinity with elemental fire as well as all other correspondences associated with that planet.

EXERCISE: CONSECRATION

The Consecration Posture is slightly different from the Command Posture, though very similar in form. In the Consecration Posture, the arm and hand are not to be visualized as a spear or sword; rather, there should be complete relaxation throughout. To prepare for the consecration, use the technique of "warming up" the hands in the Feeling the Ætheric exercise on page 75. Remember that material bases of consecrations should be thoroughly banished before charging and consecration. The item being consecrated should be wrapped or placed in a box or some other container immediately after consecration, so keep something of that kind nearby.

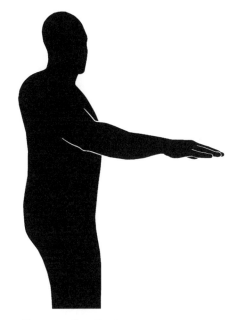

Consecration Posture

Directions

1. Relax your shoulders, keeping your elbow gently bent, and the fingers and wrist should be straight but relaxed. This posture comes in handy after projection of energy into an object, such as a talisman.

2. Perform an invocation of the specific elemental, celestial, or other energy as described in the invocation section of this chapter.

3. Place your projection hand just over the object to be consecrated without touching it.

4. After visualizing a swelling of the invoked energies in the Mercury Center, visualize the energy flowing from the Mercury Center, through the shoulder, down the arm, and out of the hand into the object. Again, the energy should be accumulated on the inhale and directed outward into the object on the exhale.

5. Feel the energy move through the projection pathway, as practiced in the circulation of energy in the Mercury Posture. Try to notice the actual sensation

of the energy moving out of the Projection Point in the center of your palm. Also note any other sensations in your hand or throughout your body.

6. Do this as many times as it takes for (1) the energy to fully pass out of the Mercury Center into the object and (2) to see the object glow. Objects infused with a particular energy will usually feature a more radiant ætheric body, and things such as talismans of a specific color or charge will typically glow their complementary color. (For instance, a red talismanic candle will glow green.)

7. Give the item a verbal charge. The charge should include what purposes for which it will be used. For example, for purifying or holy water, I might say, "Be you consecrated to the use of purification of everything upon which you are set. Be as the purifying waters of the sea and of the storm!"

8. Visualize the Projection Point closing when the energy is completely spent.

9. Close out and perform an equilibration rite (i.e., Qabalistic Cross, Calyx, or something else of your choosing).

10. Place the consecrated item inside whatever item you have set aside to wrap or put it in.

OTHER TECHNIQUES

The aforementioned techniques, while perhaps rudimentary to some degree, encompass a broad swath of essential ritual work and technique. These techniques can be incorporated and applied to the practitioner's established ritual praxis, or they can be combined. For example, warding can be followed by invocation, projection, and consecration. The basic sequential breakdown of a ritual working involves this:

1. Banishing/warding
2. Invoking/evoking
3. Working
4. Banishing/warding

The final step includes a license to depart and the reabsorption of any astral-ætheric, telesmatic images back into the body through the Mercury Center and their diffusion throughout the greater sphere of sensation of the practitioner. The following exercise is an example of a combined ritual.

EXERCISE: THE BODY TALISMAN TECHNIQUE

A person's body can be viewed as the talisman of their individual soul and spirit. In the following technique, we will charge our physical body and sphere of sensation with a specific type of force. This exercise can be done for purposes of increased energy, strength, health, and any other correspondences of the elements, planets, and zodiac.

East: Air

South: Fire

West: Water

North: Earth

Saturn: Earth

Jupiter: Air

Mars: Fire

Sun: Spirit

Venus: Earth

Mercury: Air

Moon: Water

Aries: Fire

Taurus: Earth

Gemini: Air

Cancer: Water

Leo: Fire

Virgo: Earth

Libra: Air

Scorpio: Water

Sagittarius: Fire

Capricorn: Earth

Aquarius: Air

Pisces: Water

Directions

1. Open with the Warding Rite (see page 151).

2. Perform Uniting the Above and Below (see page 92).

3. Approach the quarter associated with the particular element corresponded to the intended force to be drawn in.

4. In Command Posture, draw the invoking pentagram of the element in its corresponding color. Use the same proportions as the pentagrams of the quarters in the Warding Rite (see page 143).

5. Over the invoking pentagram, inside the void pentagonal space at its center, draw the symbol of the element, planet, or zodiacal symbol whose energy you intend to invoke.

6. Charge the center by vibrating the name(s) associated with the symbol (you can vibrate the hierarchy or chain of flow, or just keep it simple and vibrate the name of the element, planet, or zodiacal sign that the symbol represents), pointing toward the center of the pentagram in Command Posture. See it pulse with light as it is charged.

7. Use the Projection Posture to step into the symbol and then spread arms apart as in Tau Posture with feet apart so that your body stands as the pentagram.

8. In this position, breathe in and feel the energies of the pentagram being absorbed and infused into your greater sphere of sensation. Spend as much time here as you feel is needed.

9. When finished, step backward out of the pentagram and let your arms fall back at your sides. Reabsorb the ætheric energy you used to draw the pentagram through your Mercury Center.

CONCLUSION

Banishing, binding, and consecration are important ritual techniques in many systems of magic and are reliant upon the preliminary techniques given in the preceding chapter (chapter 8). The postures, techniques, and visualization utilized in the system of ætheric magic will assist in your understanding of the astral-ætheric mechanics of these operations and strengthen your overall efficacy as a magician—provided the preliminary techniques are learned and the preliminary exercises are persisted in. In order to obtain the highest yield in the more advanced work, you must have mastered the basic techniques of sensing, moving, and projecting ætheric energy.

CHAPTER 10
APPLIED TECHNIQUES

Aside from primary techniques, there are several key components to the ætheric magic system and magic in general that are integral to the comprehensive practice of magic. In this chapter, I'll discuss self-care for the practitioner and some techniques you can utilize to form your own magical self-care regimen. I'll also introduce and explain the practice of vision work and how it relates to magic. While vision work within the ætheric magic system is reduced to visualizations that accompany our exercises, there are several expanded techniques of vision work you may wish to explore throughout your magical career. I've included a section in this chapter on vision work and some exercises that can be applied to your practice.

SELF-CARE

Self-care is an often-overlooked aspect of many endeavors, magical and mundane. However, self-care is an essential part of ætheric magic because the system is predicated on the persistent and delicate balance of the ætheric energy of the practitioner, which involves maintaining good personal health. In this section, I list a series of self-care protocols to fortify the practitioner's health with techniques of ætheric recuperation and maintenance. As part of self-care must also address issues of grounding, clearing, and protection, I explain these techniques as well. The exercises in this section can be practiced as a daily, weekly, or monthly regimen or utilized specifically when needed.

A major risk of magic in general is mental and energetic burnout. The first step in preventing a complete and prolonged break in your magical endeavors is checking in with your ætheric field. To this end, we will utilize the following protocols.

EXERCISE: HANDS-ON SELF-CARE

The following exercise is a system of self-care made use of in the Japanese system of energy work known as reiki. It is a systematic checkup and recuperation of the major energy centers and organs of the practitioner's anatomy. I recommend this be done at least monthly, during the time of the waxing and full moon before sleep, since during this time there is more atmospheric (macrocosmic) ætheric energy available to all life on Earth.

Directions

1. Lying down, sitting, or standing, take a few deep breaths and bring energy into the hands. When you feel or sense they are charged, begin the exercise.

2. Place the hands palm down on top of the head, breathing deeply, and remaining relaxed. Eyes can be open or closed for this exercise. Spend as much time as you feel is needed in this posture. Make note of any thoughts, sensations, mental images, or emotions.

3. Next, lift the hands off the top of the head and place them over the face, covering the eyes. The same notes apply as previously.

4. Move down the torso in this fashion, with each successive position falling about a hand's width from the previous. Again, spend as much time as needed and take note of any sensations and any deviation from your relaxed state of body and mind.

5. At any point where energy feels blocked or there is pain, relax into the sensation using deep, rhythmic breathing, and gently ask the area what the root of the issue is. Once ascertained, you can further ask it how the blocked or stagnant energy can be freed and healed.

6. When you have reached the area of the genitals, you may stop there or move to the low back and proceed in as comfortable a way as possible upward to the back of the head. You may also return to a spot you feel might need more attention.

7. When finished, dry bathe or take a bath, and ground.

GROUNDING

The practice of magic in general is in many ways distinct from mundane experience. Practitioners spend large amounts of time cultivating faculties of imagination, focus, and will. Common exercises and practices involve vision work, dream work, astral travel, and prolonged states of meditation and visualization. In the ætheric magic system, you have also learned to tune in to and control your ætheric field, as well as learning to pull in and project that energy. These experiences, particularly when just starting out, can all contribute to feeling ungrounded. In other words, as practitioners, we are all susceptible to feeling a little disconnected from our mundane lives and even our physical bodies. Yet it is of prime importance that our daily lives and physical, as well as mental, well-being be kept in balance with all we accomplish magically. This path of dynamic equilibrium between magical development and personal well-being is the defining characteristic of an experience and mature practitioner and can only help your magic. Grounding is an important self-care technique in a healthy magical practice, and you may indeed find that you need to ground after performing some of these exercises and techniques. To help you understand when you might be feeling either grounded or ungrounded, I have listed a few examples of each.

Being grounded can have different shades of meaning for many people, since it is largely a subjective experience. However, there are some key commonalities:

- Feeling a connection to our physical bodies and immediate environments
- A moderate sense of well-being and comfortability in private and public spaces
- An ability to focus and be at least moderately present in daily circumstances
- Being in tune with general physical reality

Some feelings that indicate that you are not feeling grounded might include the following:

- Lightheadedness, dizziness
- Extreme forgetfulness, brain fog
- Mental detachment from your physical body and surroundings
- Unsure of the physical reality around you (paranoia, suspicions you are dreaming, seeing or hearing entities or voices that are not objectively present in the space)
- A sense of mania (extreme joy, sadness, any overwhelming emotion)
- A lack of ability to concentrate or the opposite—an obsession or fixation on one or several related things

In extremes of any case of feeling ungrounded, I recommend any work that you are doing (magically, ætherically, astrally) should be postponed until you have reestablished a feeling of being grounded and balanced for at least forty-eight hours. One of the ways we mitigate feelings of being ungrounded in the ætheric magic system is by first rooting ourselves with the Uniting the Above and Below exercise—the first visualization of which is rooting one-self to the earth.

Some techniques you can utilize to ground when needed are as follows:

- Eat grounding foods like nuts, tubers, roots, and carbohydrates. These foods all have a grounding effect not only on the mind but on the ætheric body as well, as they are energetically heavy. Avoid overeating, since you will likely not feel well afterward and chronic overeating after ritual may eventually develop into a habitual behavior. Also, avoid caffeine since it has a stimulating and ungrounding effect.

- Go outside and sit or lie down on the ground. This is establishing a physical connection with the earth and is a very relaxing and pleasurable way to reconnect with your surroundings and earth energy (stability) within the macrocosmic ætheric field. Walking barefoot on grass can also be an enjoyable technique to ground yourself. If weather does not permit this, you can sit or lie down on the floor of your bedroom or some other convenient spot.

- Establish a connection to the present moment. Take a few deep breaths. Look down at your feet and say to yourself, "My name is (state your name), it is (state the day of the week and full date), and I am in (state location in which you are presently)."

- Do something you enjoy that is completely unrelated to your magical practice. I like to get out and work barefoot in the garden after intense and prolonged magical workings.

If any of your symptoms are extreme or last longer than a few hours without gradually dissipating, defer to common sense and seek appropriate professional attention.

CLEARING

Clearing is another essential concept in self-care. In working with astral and ætheric energies and entities, as well as other human beings in the mundane world, it is likely that you will encounter certain negative energies that tend to permeate and stay with you. This can build up and manifest in several ways, such as feelings of discontent, anxiety, melancholy, dread, and physical pain. In this case, you want to clear the accumulated negative energy from your ætheric field. In clearing a physical space or location, a banishing or warding rite will get the job done.

One way we mitigate the accumulation of negative or unwanted energy in the ætheric magic system is in the technique of dry bathing (see page 81). This serves to clear the energetic channels and inner aura of any negative or unwanted energies that may have been picked up in interaction with physical, astral, or ætheric beings, immediately after the interaction takes place. It could be considered a technique of ætheric hygiene. I have listed another exercise that helps more intensively target and remove these energies and their associated discomforts from the body and sphere of sensation completely.

EXERCISE: THE CROWN FOUNTAIN

This technique can be utilized to move energy out of the body and sphere of sensation in instances of anxiety, pain, and other overwhelming feelings.

1. Take a few deep, centering breaths.
2. Locate the place in your body where you are holding the unwanted sensation. Grief is usually in the chest. Anxiety can be in the upper torso, abdomen, pelvic floor, throat, or face. Sexual tension is usually in the genitourinary area.
3. In any case, once you have located the area of discomfort, draw in a deep, healing breath and see the energy, whether it be pain, tension, anxiety, or otherwise, collect in the nearest alchemical center. Finally, see it accumulated there.
4. On a strong exhalation, see the collected unwanted energy shoot upward through the Middle Pillar and fountain out of the Spirit Crown Point at the top of your head. Visualize the fountain as coming out about two to three feet from the top of your head. See the unwanted energy disperse away from you like a thin cloud, being reabsorbed into the greater ætheric field to become recycled for other expressions of the æther.
5. You can end this with the Alembic exercise on page 100 and/or dry bathing.

PROTECTION

An aspect of magical practice and self-care that must be given due consideration is that of protection. "Protection against what?" I hear you ask. The magical worldview assumes that all of the physical universe is permeated by and teeming with life—both visible and invisible. This idea has obvious implications—namely, that there are hosts of unseen beings living among what we can physically see. Though disembodied intelligences cannot manifest an independent physical body, the lowest nonphysical beings can descend on the ontological chain is the ætheric level. Therefore, some of these entities will become more visible to you as you develop your ætheric sight.

I wrote in this chapter of astral gateway images, which are used to facilitate disembodied intelligences interacting with human beings on the astral plane. However, the issue of how reliable these images are is a subject of debate. Since these images are essentially astral simulacra, is it possible that malevolent or at least deceptive entities could present themselves in forms amenable to our expectations, gaining our confidence and trust under false pretenses? If a person can lie and disguise themselves, why couldn't a spirit? These questions are somewhat rhetorical in that they're meant to encourage a level of healthy skepticism and due caution in the intrepid practitioner, as well as critically examining accepted paradigms and customs in traditions of magic and psychism.

When you begin intentionally working with the astral-ætheric forces to any significant degree, you will become more active on the astral and ætheric planes and therefore become more noticeable to entities whose existence finds its ultimate expression on those planes. Warding rites such as the Lesser Banishing Ritual of the Pentagram and the Setting of the Gates given in the warding section of this chapter are effective in protecting you and the space in which you are working from interference from potentially curious entities entering into that space. However, in the physical world, we can't get someone with a bad energy and attitude to leave the room by performing a warding. Instead, we utilize the techniques of controlling the sphere of sensation and the universal voice, which we learned in chapter 7, to create an impermeable ætheric defense against astral, ætheric, and physical entities and interference.

EXERCISE: PERSONAL ÆTHERIC DEFENSE

Here is a basic exercise to help you build your defenses.

Directions

1. Take a few deep breaths, relax your body and mind, and casually assume the Middle Pillar Posture if standing or Deity-Form Posture if seated.
2. Use your rhythmic breathing and relaxed focus to tune in to your sphere of sensation.
3. Use your ætheric senses to establish that the æther is flowing.
4. Visualize around yourself the outer boundary of your sphere of sensation.

5. Once it is established in your mind's eye, visualize the outer boundary growing to about six inches thick, as we did in the Control of the Sphere of Sensation exercise (see page 99).

6. Once this is established in your mind's eye, imagine a pentagram of white light inscribed on the outer surface of your sphere of sensation in all four quarters, similar to the four pentagrams of the Lesser Ritual of the Pentagram. You do not need to physically draw these pentagrams, however—merely visualize them. This has a banishing and clearing effect in itself.

7. Once this is established, utilize the universal voice and inwardly say, "(State person or entity's name)—You cannot enter into here. You will not enter into here." If the person or entity is unknown or unspecified, simply just say, "You cannot enter into here. You will not enter into here."

8. Do this as many times as it takes for you to feel that your sphere of sensation is sealed and that no exterior influence can affect you.

9. Go about your day and remember to reduce the thickness of the aura when you have arrived at a location in which you feel comfortable and safe.

VISION WORK

In addition to self-care, there is another important tool that is an essential component of the magician's tool kit: vision work. Vision work deals with magic that takes place chiefly on the astral plane, through the mind's eye of the practitioner. Having established that the astral plane chiefly concerns the imaginal faculty, otherwise referred to as the eye of the mind, I'll now begin to elaborate on the techniques that compose vision work, including astral projection, pathworking, and scrying. This chapter will cover these essential techniques and their chief mechanism—the imaginal faculty—and show how the techniques of ætheric magic can be used to augment and amplify them.

In the Astral

The astral plane is the level of being that corresponds to the imaginal faculty and performs an intermediary role between the physical body and the level of mind. The astral plane is the first point of entry and buffer zone to the infolding layers of the interior universe. In a similar way, the sephirah of Yesod occupies a position on the Qabalistic Tree of Life linking the sephirah Malkuth (the realm of form and generation) with the sephirah Hod (the sphere of the intellectual mental processes).

The astral can be conceived as a kind of malleable level of mind that informs creation. It underlies the purely physical and works in a way similar to a living blueprint—always in motion. In magic, the astral is the meeting ground for humans and all manner of disembodied intelligences, which are referred to variously as angels, demons, and spirits, among sundry other classifications of beings. The astral plane is also the substantive ground of the imagination, both personal and collective; in Jungian language, it is the doorway to the unconscious realm of the archetypes. The astral plane is conceived as comprising two distinct levels: the lower astral plane and the higher astral plane.

Though using the imaginal faculty to access other planes and commune with metaphysical entities for any number of intentions (information, spiritual transformation, guidance, curiosity, etc.) can seem somewhat pedestrian, it's not as simple as one might imagine. The things human beings imagine, particularly if very strongly and persistently, take shape in the astral—primarily the lower astral due to its proximity to the physical-ætheric subplane—and have been referred to as "thought-forms" in the literature of nineteenth- and twentieth-century occultism, which can take on an independent existence there or be used as a gateway image appropriated by a disembodied entity.[41] Due to the presence of individual and collective thought-forms and the various entities that make it their home, the astral plane is a busy place to say the least. In fact, the astral plane could be analogized to an airport. There is high traffic comprising sojourners from near and far, and it is a meeting place—a hub for further travel. Occultists and Qabalistic magicians utilize specific structural models such as the Qabalistic Tree of Life as road maps to navigating this astral territory.

Walking the Paths

In the Qabalistic tradition, using the eye of the mind to visualize yourself traveling or walking the paths of the Tree of Life using imagery correspondent to the various natures of the paths and sephiroth in order to navigate metaphysical realms is called *pathworking*. Pathworking is essentially a form of visualization either guided by a script or informed by memorization and familiarity with the various correspondences of the paths and sephiroth on the Tree of Life. A practitioner traverses the paths that lead them to their destination—the various sephiroth. This can be done for several reasons:

---

41. Annie Besant and Charles W. Leadbeater, *Thought-Forms* (London: Theosophical Publishing House, 1901).

- Experience and training in astral visioning
- To obtain a deeper understanding of specific physical and metaphysical principles and realities through an experience of a particular sephirah (e.g., Yesod is attributed to the sphere of dreams, images, intuition, and the unconscious)
- To commune with a specific metaphysical hierarchy of beings associated with a particular sephirah
- To gain insight into the relationship between different parts of the tree and astral plane in general
- Spiritual transformation as a product of all the aforementioned

EXERCISE: ENTERING THE UNDERWORLD (A PATHWORKING)

In an effort to engage in some basic astral vision work, we'll be performing a pathworking consisting of traveling from the sephirah of Malkuth to the sephirah of Yesod by way of the path that connects them—the Path of Saturn. This path is also referred to among Qabalistic magicians as the underworld. It exemplifies the experience of entering into the astral plane and traversing it from lower to higher, entering into the sephirah of Yesod and returning the way you came, back to Malkuth.

Find a comfortable place to begin this exercise, preferably sitting upright in a position that is comfortable, but not so comfortable that you are likely to fall asleep. You may want to either have someone read this to you or record yourself reading it and play it back during the actual performance of the pathworking.

Begin Pathworking

Relax your body, take a few deep breaths, and close your eyes. Imagine standing in a temple with ten walls and a stone altar at its center. The lighting is dim and the temperature is cool within the temple, and you feel a slight breeze blowing from an entrance you cannot see. You hear echoes of trickling water and crackling fire reverberating off the walls, and these you cannot visually locate either. A beautiful angel stands across the altar from you in white robes, with long blonde hair. Their name is Sandalphon, angel of the terrestrial sphere of Earth. Greeting you with a smile and a nod, Sandalphon steps aside and gestures toward a black curtain at the furthest end of the temple directly before you.

You walk together toward the curtain, and as it comes more clearly into view, you see the planetary symbol of Saturn embroidered in violet thread upon the thick curtain. The lower part of the symbol seems to reflect a silver glint. You recognize it as a scythe.

Sandalphon steps forward and slowly pulls back the curtain, revealing a stone entryway leading to impenetrable darkness. A chill wind hits you hard, and for a second you hear the ghastly moans of many voices carried upon that wind. Sandalphon gestures for you to step forward into the darkness. For a moment, you balk, but then you take heart as Sandalphon places their hand gently upon your shoulder and smiles, reviving your courage. You step forward a few paces, entering the threshold. The darkness beyond is utterly silent. You take another step and fall forward through the darkness, as if the corridor were suddenly shifted completely vertically. You pass into a state of sleep for a few moments.

When you awake, the light of the sun is dim, casting rays of red and purple across the sky. All you can see are the beautiful colors of its rays; the disc of sun remains out of view. You become vaguely aware that you are on the deck of a boat—you feel wooden boards beneath you and the gentle rocking motion of a body of water beneath the boat. Sitting up, you look around and see that the boat is floating on a river from whose banks grow tall palm trees and exotic foliage. Suddenly, you hear footsteps approaching from behind you. You turn to see who approaches, and a strangely dressed being in an odd posture comes into view. He is tall and slender and wears a brightly colored yellow, red, and blue apron at his waist, with matching wristbands and collar. His arms are raised to shoulder length, bent at the elbows with his forearms pointing straight upward in a U-shaped position. This is Heka—the ancient Egyptian god of magic. He seems to be waiting for you to rise.

As you rise to your feet, Heka turns around and begins walking toward the other end of the long, flat ship deck. You follow him. Heka leads you to an entourage of other divine beings—the deities who accompany the Egyptian sun god Ra on his solar barque. The company of gods is facing west, where the purple-red rays of the sun's light are just barely visible in the sky. The deities keep their eye on the horizon, and you watch as the last rays of sunset fade from their somber and statuesque faces. They are preparing to enter *amenti*, the west gate of the *duat*—the Egyptian underworld. As the darkness of night descends, you notice that you are no longer floating on the river. Now, you are floating through a star-studded darkness resembling outer space. You feel that you are now well beyond the terrestrial sphere of Earth.

A thick fog suddenly overtakes the boat. The retinue of deities stands stoically at the bow of the ship now silhouetted by the dense fog. You feel its dense clouds against your face as the boat begins to slow down, as if meeting resistance. The screech of a hawk comes from behind you, and you turn to see a hawk-headed god with fierce eyes at the ship's steering wheel. With a quarter turn of the wheel, you feel the ship turn and then suddenly drop as if the floor beneath you had given out. For a moment, the boat is in free fall.

Suddenly, the boat regains stability, landing upon what feels like semi-pliant ground. The boat creeks forward, and you hear moans and groans coming from what sounds like beneath the barque. You approach the edge, carefully, and peer over to see a sea of ghostly figures with dusty faces and glossy eyes, moving the boat forward with their hands, passing its weight forward like someone crowd surfing. You look around at the ship's crew of deities. They remain unperturbed—focused on the darkness ahead. You detect in their faces a faint expression of anticipation. Then, you see something in the distance. It is a great gateway—a pair of twin pylons resembling two enormous Egyptian lotuses. As you pass between them, the ship seems to regain its previous sensation of buoyancy. Looking outward into the darkness, you begin to hear the soft sound of gentle waves lapping against the boat's sides. It appears as if you are back on a river, except now it is the dark of night.

You look up at the clear night sky and see what appears to be the milky way. As you continue to peer at the large band of bright, clustered stars, you notice faint outlines of a feminine body. The band of overhead stars seems to form a massive archway stretching from the horizon in front of you to the horizon directly behind you. Straight above your head you notice two stars directly in line with one another, shining much more brightly than the others. You are filled with a feeling of curiosity and wonder. Suddenly, the stars flash and reveal themselves to be eyes!

A thunderous female voice sounds from the sky, seeming to shake the very sphere of the heavens. "Child of the Night of Time," she says, addressing you. "I am Nuit and the moon is my womb. All things that come into being must pass through me, to be born upon the shores of the temporal Nile—the river of Time. I am ever pregnant, carrying in me all ideas soon to take form. I am Isis as she gestates and I am the celestial river of night, through which souls swim to earthly destinations. In me, they find life and rest, the darkness of night and brightness of stars. You commune with me in your dreams, where I am fertile and hidden. Take heart! For the time of the dawn light is not far off, though you now pass by the shores of midnight among the retinue of noble gods who dutifully watch and wait in fortitude for the hour when the sleeper shall awaken." At these last words, you feel the hard and blunt sensation of the boat hitting the shore. You look to the deities for your cue to fear or relief. They gesture that you must deboard onto the dark shore.

You step off with your guide Heka, who guides you further inland. Peering through the quiet night all around you, you see the fires of a temple in the distance. Arriving at the enormous, violet temple door, you are stopped by two jackal-headed guards holding swords that glint with silver light. Heka turns to you and says, "We arrive at the temple of the moon." After a moment, the doors of the temple swing open, and you and your guide Heka enter. The temple is round within, and around its circumference are arrayed nine lotus-shaped pillars. In the center of the temple is a tall, slender altar made of moonstone, with a silver basin filled with clear, still water atop it. Dim flames flicker from torches ensconced in each pillar, and through a circular skylight in the center of the temple dome, moonlight pours down over the altar. Heka gestures for you to approach the altar. You take a few steps toward it and notice the silhouette of a feminine figure standing across the altar from you.

As you walk up to the altar's edge, only the figure's eyes become visible to you. You cannot tell if they are illuminated by slivers of moonlight falling in from the skylight or if they are radiating by their own light. A voice smooth as velvet asks, "What do you see?" Confusion comes over you for a moment. You struggle to understand the question. Then, almost involuntarily, you blurt out, "Darkness!" The figure's eyes look down at the basin, seemingly gesturing toward it. You lean forward and peer into the clear water within the basin. The moonlight gives it a glimmer that almost makes it sparkle. You faintly become aware of your own reflection. Leaning closer, you peer into your reflection's eyes, becoming entranced for a moment. The translucent shape of Heka begins to form around your reflection, yet you are not startled—you persist in your gaze.

The eyes of the translucent figure of Heka align and merge with your own eyes in the reflective water, and you begin to feel a whirling sensation, like breath or a breeze blowing directly upon your brow in the space of the third eye between and slightly above your eyebrows. You lean into this feeling, closing your eyes.

Take a moment at this point of the pathworking to allow any thoughts, images, words, or sensations to organically appear in your mind, making a mental note of them. You open your eyes in the vision, and the figure on the other side of the altar has disappeared. You look around and so has Heka, but the door of the temple is open and a cool night breeze blows in to the temple.

You retrace your steps through the temple and exit through the door. The jackal-headed guards gesture for you to follow the road by which you arrived at the temple.

You traverse the road back to the shore where the boat awaits you. Its retinue of gods welcome you, and you notice Heka is not among them. You think it must be early morning because the faint haze of dawn light is beginning to push back the darkness. The boat pushes off and heads directly toward the eastern horizon. You think about your journey and feel as though the words and experiences have been absorbed into the very fabric of your being. As the sun mounts the horizon, you look over the side of the boat into the illuminated waters and see your reflection. You *are* Heka. The sunlight washes out the reflection with its brightness, and you turn to face it. The solar disc, now fully clear of the horizon, is enormous, taking up most of the visible sky before you. As you stand before it in the company of the noble deities, you realize you stand before a god—Ra. As Ra's light washes out everything in your field of vision with white light, you feel the welcoming warmth of his rays against your face.

You open your eyes, and you are back in the temple of Malkuth—the temple of the elements. Sandalphon smiles at you from across the stone altar. You look down at your hands and feet and see that you have resumed your usual body. You bid Sandalphon farewell and exit the temple.

Take a few deep breaths and gently wiggle your fingers and toes, returning to the room in which you physically sit. When you are ready, open your eyes. Immediately journal any thoughts, sensations, or experiences.

SCRYING

The term *scry* comes from a shortening of the archaic English word *descry*, meaning "to see."[42] Scrying is a type of vision work utilizing the imaginal faculty similar to how it is used in pathworking, without the strictly Qabalistic diagram of the Tree of Life as the foundation dictating specific correspondences and symbolism. Therefore, it can be closer to mediumism than pathworking, rendering the practitioner in a less deliberate and more receptive state for longer.

Historically, scrying has been accomplished by gazing into a reflective surface of some kind, usually a block stone—typically onyx or another stone having a mirrorlike surface when polished—until reaching a trancelike state where one can begin to tap into the astral gateway images appearing before the eye of the mind. Stones, mirrors, and bowls of water were used as focal points, rather than merely closing one's eyes and potentially becoming prone to the distractions of the discursive internal monologue. I recommend using specific symbols, such as those of the elements, the planets, the zodiac, and the major arcana of the tarot, in order to scry more intentionally.

EXERCISE: CONSTRUCTING SCRYING CARDS

I will give the basic steps to entry-level scrying. However, the resultant vision work is not as guided as pathworking, so I will leave it to you to employ the technique and record your results. You can either buy a tarot deck (if you've already got one, feel free to use that), or construct scrying cards for the elements, planets, or zodiac. This can be done simply and affordably with a set of colored pencils or markers and index cards.

Directions

1. Find the corresponding color to the particular element, planet, or zodiacal sign as given in the list on page 121 and use this to draw the symbol.
2. On the blank side of the index card, draw as neatly and symmetrically as possible the symbol of the element, planet, or zodiacal sign you are intending to scry. Do not make the figures so small that you have to strain to see them if you are sitting a few feet away from the card.

---

42. Online Etymology Dictionary, s.v. "scry (v.)," by Douglas Harper, accessed September 13, 2024, https://www.etymonline.com/search?q=scry.

3. If you have used a marker, set the index card aside face up after drawing the symbol and allow the marker ink to dry before using it or putting it away. This will ensure the card does not become smudged.

4. When the cards are dry, keep them together in an appropriate container, such as a small card box, or wrapped in a piece of linen. You can bind them together with a rubber band or some twine.

EXERCISE: ENTERING THE ASTRAL GATEWAY

The image(s) you use in scrying will serve as a gateway to the astral environment of the symbol itself—the aspect of the astral plane that is associated with the nature of the particular element, planet, or zodiacal sign. Keep in mind that we learned (in chapter 7) about how all the aforementioned are conceived as the constituent creative potencies of the manifest universe and therefore express ideas in the Divine Mind.

I recommend spending some time looking at the particular card and studying and understanding the various associations and correspondences of its symbol(s). This will help these related ideas more firmly root in your conscious and subconscious minds, generating a more reliable and internally consistent experience of the symbol's astral environs. Last, perform this exercise in a comfortable and quiet place where you will not be disturbed. I also recommend that this exercise be done seated for purposes of safety. If you nod off or become disoriented while standing with your eyes closed, a fall could result.

Directions

1. Place the symbol to be used in a vertical position on your altar. A bifold picture stand from your local arts and crafts store is a suitable and affordable item for this purpose.

2. Be sure there is enough light in the room so that the symbol is visible.

3. Sit comfortably yet remaining alert, approximately three to four feet from the card, which should be as in your direct line of sight as possible.

4. Take a few deep breaths to center yourself, and then gaze at the symbol for as long as you can without blinking. Thirty to sixty seconds is preferable.

5. Close your eyes and see the symbol upon an enormous gate, door, or curtain—whatever suits your preference—in the eye of your mind.

6. When you have firmly established this image in the eye of your mind, pass through the door or gate and into the astral environment of the symbol.

7. Take note of what you experience there. You may stay put and look around, or venture deep into the territory of the symbol. Always be sure to leave breadcrumbs—that is, make sure you retrace your steps back to the door to exit the vision when you are finished.

8. Come back to the room in which you physically sit slowly, and immediately journal your experiences.

ÆTHERIC VISION WORK

As mentioned earlier, stimulation and use of the third eye and astral sight can be affected by the geometric pattern of energy that forms in the Sulfur Posture, which stimulates the third eye. Therefore, we can utilize this posture to prepare for vision work such as scrying, astral travel, and pathworking. While the details and mechanics of such vision work is beyond the scope of this book, there is a good amount of practical resources that can be affordably obtained on the subject, which you may pair with these techniques and exercises. In its essence, astral vision work differs from ætheric sight in that the images are formed in the imaginal faculty. Yet there is a distinct sense of location or place when we are working on the astral, so to speak. However, the mental forms we perceive at this interior level of reality are of a very fluid and tenuous nature, and therefore it is necessary to build constructs within which to work. A great example of this is in pathworking using the diagram of the Tree of Life. Another is tattva scrying, which was developed at length by the early Hermetic Order of the Golden Dawn.

EXERCISE: OPENING THE THIRD EYE

This basic exercise corresponds to and is a further extension of our pathworking to the temple of the moon in Yesod in the exercise on page 171. It serves to awaken the energy of the third eye and can work extremely effectively as a preliminary to any kind of vision work. However, the inner lights may persist in waking vision, which is not necessarily a bad thing, but it may cause some distraction and irritation to some practitioners. The best way to mitigate this is to perform a grounding act, such as having a meal, immediately afterward.

The Sulfur Posture triangle serves as a kind of focal point for energy, as well as a viewfinder for astral-ætheric sight. Remember that these planes are related, particularly the lower astral and ætheric—what the mind molds in the astral, with strong focus, affects the molding of the ætheric light. It is important in some instances, as in the projection of a telesmatic image, that ætheric light should be reabsorbed into the ætheric body by envisioning the beam of light projecting from the Mercury/Tiphareth Center as reverting back into it, being reabsorbed into the Salt Center, and diffused into the sphere of sensation.

If you are using this technique to astral travel, the triangle formed by the hands in Sulfur Posture can be used like a gateway by visualizing the intended scenery within the triangle and projecting a beam from the Third Eye Point into the landscape. Move your consciousness down this beam of light and into the landscape.

Keep in mind that during the following exercise, as with all the exercises given in this work, it is of utmost importance to achieve and maintain a state of deep relaxation while remaining present with internal imagery. The tendency may be to fall asleep, so avoid getting too comfortable. Relaxation *can* be achieved in an upright posture; it just takes practice! If you do fall asleep, get some rest and try again tomorrow.

Directions

1. Sit in Deity-Form Posture, taking several deep, rhythmic breaths. Box breathing may be useful for regulating the breath for this kind of exercise.

2. When you have achieved a relaxed and alert state, slowly elevate your arms and hands to Sulfur Posture, with the tips of the thumbs and index finger gently touching. Experiment with distance between hands and the Third Eye Point (between the eyebrows) and note any accompanying visuals or sensations.

3. Imagine a spiral of energy forming at the Third Eye Point, extending out through the center of the triangle formed by your hands. Hold this for a short while and bring your awareness to the Third Eye Point. Relax into any sensation you may begin to feel. Don't try to analyze it. It is key that you remain relaxed.

4. Continue to breathe deeply and concentrate on cultivating the inner vision. At first, this will likely engage your physical eyesight, which will only perceive the darkness of your closed eyelids. Relax into alert awareness without striving to perceive anything with the physical eyes. This may take several minutes—even several sessions—but persist, and it will happen. In time, the

"inner lights" will become visible, swirling, undulating, and dancing. The most common of these has been referred to as the "blue flame." It is also often accompanied by a swirling or buzzing sensation at the Third Eye Point. The tendency is to furrow the brow in hyperfixation on this point. Keep your face and awareness relaxed. Have no great care for results; just remain engaged in the practice, and results will come.

5. Cultivate this sensation not by forcing it or reengaging the discursive mind, but by bringing gentle awareness to it while relaxing into the sensation.

6. In this field of interior mental vision, visualize a pentagram glowing with white light. Focus and hold it there.

7. When it is established, slowly open your eyes without losing focus on the visualized pentagram. See it strongly in the triangle formed by your thumbs and index fingers. Once again, experiment with distance, bringing it closer and further away from the face, keeping your focus on the visualized pentagram.

8. Close your eyes, then open them, visualizing the pentagram in red flame now. Close your eyes again, and visualize the pentagram in yellow flame, then blue, then black. Finally, close your eyes, seeing the pentagram fade completely from vision.

9. Close the Third Eye Point down, and center any energy you have accumulated in your Mercury Center.

Sulfur Scrying Posture

CONCLUSION

The techniques given here can be applied as needed. My recommendation is that you engage in the self-care protocols often (two to three times per week) starting off, to help get more in tune with your own body and ætheric field. The scrying and vision work techniques will help hone your visualization abilities and broaden your magical and psychic abilities in general. Pathworking in particular will cultivate a profound level of insight and connection to the Qabalistic Tree of Life. The techniques and postures of ætheric magic can be utilized to assist and deepen your experience in the inner worlds.

CHAPTER 11
DEVELOPING A PRACTICE

I will now finally begin to outline a program of practice that will serve as a road map or progress plan in developing your skills in sensing and moving ætheric energy. This should also assist in expediting the alchemy of the elemental self and incorporating the techniques of ætheric magic into your own practice. It is not necessary to outline a detailed course of practice, because part of the function of this system is to allow you, the practitioner, to experience it for yourself and use it for your own needs. Therefore, I'll be highlighting a few core exercises and techniques in alignment with a daily, weekly, monthly, and yearly cycle of practice.

We'll begin by focusing on the most immediate diurnal cycle of day and night. Experiment with what time of day or night and what level of lighting works best for your exercises in learning to see ætheric energy. Remember that it is not visualization—it is *perception*, and success in this respect is dependent upon being able to relax the body, mind, and vision.

You can utilize the planetary day and hour (sun for spirit or fire) or the ætheric tides (again, sunrise being the hour of spirit/quintessence) to time your exercises for optimal effect. My recommendation is to eat as cleanly as possible (i.e., minimal processed foods and sugars) while undergoing this period of early development, since an elevated presence of toxins may make the process more difficult. I would also recommend the practitioner not eat too heavily before any energy work, especially a long ritual. Regardless of what you choose to do—press on!

TIMING TECHNIQUES: THE DAYS, HOURS, AND TIDES

Timing techniques are extremely beneficial in enhancing the power and efficacy of all ritual, magical, and healing work. Our timing techniques consist of three parts: planetary days and hours and the ætheric tides.

Each day of the week corresponds to one of the seven classical planetary bodies that govern or influence it. The planets in turn have their own corresponding elemental attributes.

Day	Planetary Body	Element
Sunday	Sun	Fire/Spirit
Monday	Moon	Water
Tuesday	Mars	Fire
Wednesday	Mercury	Air
Thursday	Jupiter	Air
Friday	Venus	Earth
Saturday	Saturn	Earth

Further, the days have their own planetary hours beginning at sunrise of that day and starting with the planet of the day (e.g., the hour of the sun is at sunrise on a Sunday). These hours are not proper "hours" as we think of them but equal divisions of daylight from sunrise to sunset. There are several reliable apps that calculate and give us the planetary hours on demand. With this, we have a day-and-hour formula for the specific timing of planetary, zodiacal (based on planetary rulerships), and elemental workings.

The Planetary Hours

Sunrise (1)	2	3	4	5	6	7	8	9	10	11	12
Saturday Saturn	Jupiter	Mars	Sun	Venus	Mercury	Moon	Saturn	Jupiter	Mars	Sun	Venus
Sunday Sun	Venus	Mercury	Moon	Saturn	Jupiter	Mars	Sun	Venus	Mercury	Moon	Saturn
Monday Moon	Saturn	Jupiter	Mars	Sun	Venus	Mercury	Moon	Saturn	Jupiter	Mars	Sun
Tuesday Mars	Sun	Venus	Mercury	Moon	Saturn	Jupiter	Mars	Sun	Venus	Mercury	Moon
Wednesday Mercury	Moon	Saturn	Jupiter	Mars	Sun	Venus	Mercury	Moon	Saturn	Jupiter	Mars
Thursday Jupiter	Mars	Sun	Venus	Mercury	Moon	Saturn	Jupiter	Mars	Sun	Venus	Mercury
Friday Venus	Mercury	Moon	Saturn	Jupiter	Mars	Sun	Venus	Mercury	Moon	Saturn	Jupiter

Sunset (13)	14	15	16	17	18	19	20	21	22	23	24
Mercury	Moon	Saturn	Jupiter	Mars	Sun	Venus	Mercury	Moon	Saturn	Jupiter	Mars
Jupiter	Mars	Sun	Venus	Mercury	Moon	Saturn	Jupiter	Mars	Sun	Venus	Mercury
Venus	Mercury	Moon	Saturn	Jupiter	Mars	Sun	Venus	Mercury	Moon	Saturn	Jupiter
Saturn	Jupiter	Mars	Sun	Venus	Mercury	Moon	Saturn	Jupiter	Mars	Sun	Venus
Sun	Venus	Mercury	Moon	Saturn	Jupiter	Mars	Sun	Venus	Mercury	Moon	Saturn
Moon	Saturn	Jupiter	Mars	Sun	Venus	Mercury	Moon	Saturn	Jupiter	Mars	Sun
Mars	Sun	Venus	Mercury	Moon	Saturn	Jupiter	Mars	Sun	Venus	Mercury	Moon

There is another system taken from the tattva tradition of the ancient Tamil Siddhas of India. This is the system of the *tattvic tides*. The tattvas are the qualitative elemental permutations of æther, called *akasa* in the Vedic system, and correspond to which element has a predominance during a specific period of time. These ætheric elemental cycles are conceived of as tides in that they ebb and flow due to their mixed nature. It is the underlying akasa that is the substrate or container within which these elements exist in mixture, each coming to the fore, so to speak, during a tattvic hour. In our system, we refer them to the Western five-element system of spirit/quintessence, air, fire, water, and earth. The tattva system was one of the earliest systems of energy we know of.

The tattvic or ætheric tides begin at midnight and always begin with the fifth element of spirit and end with the element of earth. Throughout a two-hour cycle, the tides move from spirit (akasa) to air (*vayu*), air to fire (*tejas*), fire to water (*apas*), and water to earth (*prithivi*) with each complete cycle. The governing element of each two-hour cycle represents the dominant tattva. Within these two-hour cycles there is another cycle of what are called sub-tattvas, which alternate in the same order (spirit to air, air to fire, fire to water, water to earth) every twenty-four minutes. So for instance, the third sub-tattva of the spirit (akasa) cycle is fire (tejas), yielding the tattvic tide of fire of spirit (tejas of akasa).

I have found a combination of these three considerations for timing a ritual or healing exercise is one of the most powerful tools in my magical tool kit. It is recommended that the practitioner experiment with these for themselves and record the effects. Remember to keep in mind the lunar cycles as well, as these have an effect on the volume and availability of the ætheric tides.

The Tattvic Tides

Tattvic Hour (2 Hours)	Sub-Tattva 1: Akasha (24 mins)	Sub-Tattva 2: Vayu (24 mins)	Sub-Tattva 3: Tejas (24 mins)	Sub-Tattva 4: Apas (24 mins)	Sub-Tattva 5: Prithivi (24 mins)
Akasha (Sunrise)	Akasha-akasha	Akasha-vayu	Akasha-tejas	Akasha-apas	Akasha-prithivi
Vayu	Vayu-akasha	Vayu-vayu	Vayu-tejas	Vayu-apas	Vayu-prithivi
Tejas	Tejas-akasha	Tejas-vayu	Tejas-tejas	Tejas-apas	Tejas-prithivi
Apas	Apas-akasha	Apas-vayu	Apas-tejas	Apas-apas	Apas-prithivi
Prithivi	Prithivi-akasha	Prithivi-vayu	Prithivi-tejas	Prithivi-apas	Prithivi-prithivi

PRACTICAL CONSIDERATIONS

For those completely new to energy work, I recommend practicing the Uniting the Above and Below exercise (see page 92) once a week for two to four weeks before proceeding to more frequent practice and complex exercises. It is important to examine how the influx and movement of energy is affecting the psyche-ætheric makeup of your elemental self. We want to avoid burnout or overwhelm. If you are a relatively experienced practitioner, I recommend a daily regimen of this exercise shortly after waking. The exercise at about a medium pace should only take about twenty to twenty-five minutes total. Once this has been mastered, regular practice of the warding rite should begin once a day for one week depending on individual progress. After this, it could be practiced once in the morning shortly after waking and once in the evening before bed.

The practice of working with the Sulfur Center to activate the Third Eye Point and perform vision work is typically best performed at night, whereas active energy movement though the Middle Pillar and sphere of sensation is best during the day. This is because the movement of energy in this manner will typically energize a practitioner, and the influence of the moon on the lunar half of the ætheric tides is usually conducive to vision work. Working ætheric energy in this way, as mentioned before, will affect the elemental self and can produce a much more active and vivid dream life. It may be useful to keep your magical journal near your bedside in order to be able to record any significant experiences in dreams.

The practitioner should then perform invocations of specific elements on corresponding planetary days once per week. For instance, they could perform an invocation of fire during the hour of Mars on a Tuesday; they could utilize the ætheric tide of fire—two hours after sunrise—on a Tuesday as well, remembering to center and balance the energies in their Mercury Center. This should be practiced for an average of four months, focusing on one element per month, totaling in a minimum of four elemental invocations per month on average. This will effect an assimilation of these energies and help us call to the fore and delineate the "elements within."

After this, a period of at least one month should be spent invoking spirit/quintessence through the planetary body of the sun (the hour of the sun on a Sunday). This should be combined with the alchemical circulations of the light, again focusing on centering the energy in the Mercury/Tiphareth Center, utilizing the elemental Middle Pillar.

From here the rest of the planets can begin to be invoked once a day utilizing the appropriate day-and-hour combination or whenever the practitioner sees fit. From here, zodiacal invocations could be started, using the appropriate planetary day based on the scheme of planetary rulerships. Planetary rulerships are a system of correspondences based on a second-century Hellenistic astrological schematic referred to as the *Thema Mundi*, or birth of the universe. This table delineates the rationale for specific zodiacal signs being ruled or governed by particular planetary bodies. Aside from the two luminaries of sun and moon, each planet has a day house and a night house.

These distinctions represent the active or receptive polarity of the planetary body's expression and can also be used to time specific invocations. Again, it is advantageous to perform ritual workings with a knowledge of where the actual planets and constellations relevant to the work are positioned in the sky. In our system, we will focus primarily on the seven classical planets of antiquity, as they correspond to the six sephiroth below Da'ath, inclusive of Da'ath, representing the influence of the Supernal Triad through the planet Saturn. In the Qabalistic system of the parts of the soul, this corresponds to the individual's *ruach* ("spirit"/"breath") or inner self, corresponding to the Yetziratic World of Formation in the Four World model. This is juxtaposed just above the Nephesch and G'uph, or ætheric and dense physical bodies. These also correspond to the Hexagram Rituals of planetary magic. Again, the practitioner may choose to include the outer planets as they see fit.

Planetary Rulerships		
Planet	**Day House**	**Night House**
Saturn	Aquarius	Capricorn
Jupiter	Sagittarius	Pisces
Mars	Aries	Scorpio
Sun	Leo	
Venus	Taurus	Virgo
Mercury	Gemini	Libra
Moon		Cancer

THE WHEEL OF THE YEAR

A further way to incorporate the assimilation of the forces of the elements, planets, and zodiac is to sync your work to the Wheel of the Year. The Wheel of the Year is a circular model representing the cyclical nature of the seasons, lunar cycles, and the year as a whole. It is a foundational model within modern witchcraft as well as ceremonial magic. Synching your work to the Wheel of the Year would take the form of planetary and zodiacal invocations based on the months and the signs of the zodiac, corresponding to the seasons.

The Wheel of the Year and the zodiac correspond to one another in an intimate way. The seasons in the Northern Hemisphere reflect the attributes of the zodiacal signs and their ruling planets. For instance, Aries, ruled by Mars, represents cardinal, initiatory energies of warmth and vitality at the vernal equinox; Capricorn, ruled by Saturn, represents a slow and steady perseverance of the onset of the cold and dark of winter. To this end, zodiacal talismans can be made utilizing the components and techniques listed in chapter 7 for use in the transformation of the sphere of sensation and further ritual and magical uses.

While there are no absolutely necessary physical items, such as wands, swords, or other ritual implements, in ætheric magic, the system itself provides a circuitry comprising a full complement of universal energies. These energies can be invoked just prior to the construction of various ritual tools, such as wands, candles, talismans, and tinctures, to name but a few. These can also be invoked to charge the sphere of sensation for work such as invocation; prayer; contemplation; elemental, planetary, or zodiacal pathworkings; exorcisms; laboratory alchemical operations; speaking; teaching engagements; and so on. You will find that these can be applied to virtually any task or scenario. Once these techniques have been mastered, they can be done internally, virtually anywhere. It is a system of power on demand—the spiritual circuitry of the macrocosm, accessible from within the microcosm.

Further, you could work with these centers and energies along another alchemical line—by directing the flow and sequencing of the movement of æther with corresponding alchemical operations. For instance, calcination could take place by stimulating the fiery sensation, awakening the Third Eye Point and the Sulfur Center, and then using the Middle Pillar (centerline of body) to bring that red, fiery energy to the Malkuth Center (feet and ground). From there, the practitioner could use the heat to perform a distillation, heating the Salt/Water/Yesod Center (pelvic region) with that earthy fire generating a vapor, which, passing through the Da'ath Center of elemental air, generating the mother sound of aleph (*ahhh*), rises again to the Sulfur Center, to collect in the ambix of the Sulfur Center as distillate. A final example is in the operation of sublimation, whereby all previous centers having been awakened and permuted with one another are balanced, gathered, and prepared for use in the Mercury/Tiphareth Center (center of chest). Again, the ætheric tides or planetary days and hours could be utilized with great profit here.

CRAFTING YOUR RITUALS

As part of a complete system, you, the ætheric magic practitioner, are offered methods of designing your own personalized rituals. You will be able to apply every single technique, exercise, and development of knowledge, context, and skill in sensing and working with ætheric energy to both your magical and mundane lives. If you are new to magic, everything you've learned in this book so far will put you on excellent footing to become an effective and confident ritual magician. I encourage everyone who reads this book and works the ætheric magic system to read and experiment widely in traditions of magic. This is how we develop a personal style and how magic becomes more than something you do and becomes what you *are*.

The following exercises are some examples of how you can put together a ritual from your previously learned techniques and exercises, which you should be ready to perform mostly from memory at this point. If you need a memory aid, you could write the sequencing out and keep it nearby on a music stand or end table.

A ritual is typically structured in the same way a theatrical play or piece of music is—in three parts. These consist of an opening, working, and closing. It's important, however, that we see these techniques, exercises, and parts not as completely separate sections but rather as one continuous whole smoothly blending together in an organic way, like a dance perhaps. Part two in our example will involve the invocation of the planetary energies of Venus and their projection into a consecrated Venusian talisman. Part two, however, can be tweaked, added to, or exchanged for any other ritual working the practitioner desires. This will serve as a simple example of invocation, projection, and sealing of the ætheric energy of a planet into an object.

Preparation for Ritual

Your ritual space should ideally be a separate room where you will not be disturbed. There should be some kind of altar in the center of the space with enough room to walk around. If this is not feasible, then you can turn in place for any necessary changes in direction. If you are using candles, make sure you have a fire extinguisher at a quickly accessible location. Any material basis for a talismanic consecration or any other form of astrological or elemental magic should be at the ready. I like to wrap mine in silk or linen until the consecration begins.

If it is also unfeasible to vibrate words of power or divine names, you can use the universal voice technique, and when giving the talisman its charge, you may speak in hushed tones, retaining a spirit of command. Before the ritual begins, be sure to know where in the sky the zodiacal constellation, section of the ecliptic, and/or planet you will be utilizing is in relation to the position of the center of the room in which you will be working. A good preliminary to ritual is a short period of silence and a period of meditation or prayer.

EXERCISE: RITUAL BATH

Ritual baths work very well in clearing any unwanted energies that have built up over the course of the day and do not seem to be easily cleared.

Directions

1. Run the water and allow the tub to fill so that most of your body is submerged when you are in it.

2. Before getting into the tub, invoke Highest Deity and then stand in Command Posture, with your hand pointed directly at the water.

3. In a loud and powerful voice say, "Creature of Water! I exorcise you of all unwanted energies—I purge you for the work of purification!"

4. Draw a banishing pentagram over the surface of the water and then hold your projection hand palm down over the water in Consecration Posture. After each aspect of God/Goddess, slowly draw an equal-armed cross over the water with your open palm.

5. Say, "In the Name of God/Godess the Creator/trix (+), in the Name of God/Goddess the Created (+), and in the Name of the Ineffable Spirit (+), I consecrate you in service to this work. Fiat! Fiat! Fiat!"

6. Draw an invoking spirit pentagram over the water.

7. Proceed to the ritual bath.

8. Use a clean towel to dry off before dressing for ritual.

Invoking Spirit Pentagram

Note

You could also exorcise and consecrate some salt for use in the ritual bath by the same method, substituting "Creature of Earth" where appropriate.

EXERCISE: RITUAL FOR A VENUSIAN TALISMAN

Consecrating a Venusian talisman (or a talisman charged and consecrated to the planet Venus) is a ritualized process that produces an extremely useful magical implement. The attributes and correspondences of the planet Venus can be invoked on demand with this talisman, bringing in love, sensuality, greenery, stability, and balance to the life of its owner.

The following ritual comes in three parts. You will first perform an opening. Openings are important because they set the tone and provide us with a sterile field and boundaries of our magical container within which to work. It also helps the mind begin shifting into the necessary state of focused, relaxed awareness, which is necessary for activating and moving ætheric energy for the purposes of ritual magic.

The second part is the working, which is the portion within the ritual that the actual intended magical work is performed. The conditions leading up to this— the timing, the preparation (such as the Three Centers Distillation or equilibrating rite), the warding—should all create a moment of opportunity within which to enact your magical event.

The final part is the closure, or the ending of the ritual.

Directions: The Opening

1. Begin your ritual by first achieving a relaxed, balanced, and focused state. Assume Middle Pillar Posture, and following a few deep, centering breaths, perform the Uniting Above and Below exercise.

2. Root deeply into the earth, pulling up the receptive energy of celestial salt, open up to the stars, and draw in the active force of celestial sulfur. Combine these in the alembic of your heart—the Mercury Center.

3. Once the pathways are open and your ætheric energy is balanced and circulating, you will proceed to an invocation to your highest idea of deity. This can be one of the openings listed in the previous chapter, or feel free to open with whatever invocation you prefer or feel most called to. Whichever you choose, remember to center and ground the energy once again in your Mercury Center with the Quintessence Posture. Feel it centered within you, balancing and strengthening you.

4. Next, proceed to the warding ritual, using the Projection Posture and Stop Posture when needed. Make sure to complete a full circle of your working space utilizing Command Posture with your projection hand before returning to the center of the space and invoking the guardians of the quarters.

5. Your space now open and ready for working, proceed to declare an intention for this ritual. For instance, it could be something like, "I declare this space cleared, guarded, and ready for ritual." Or more explicitly, "I declare this space cleared and guarded for the purpose of consecrating a Venusian talisman!"

Directions: The Working

1. The working should be preceded by some kind of centering exercise, such as a Three Centers Distillation, or a shorter gathering of energy into the Mercury Center using the Quintessence Posture; deep, directing breaths; and visualization.

2. Next, unveil your material to be consecrated as a talisman and place it on the center of your altar. Assume Command Posture, trace a Triangle of Art around it, and exorcise the object using the same formula as given in the rit-

ual bath section, substituting "Creature of Earth" if the object is a solid rather than a liquid.

3. This complete, take a few breaths, move or turn so that you are facing the quarter of the sky where the celestial body is located, and assume Invocation Posture.

4. Envision your sphere of sensation very clearly in either white or gold. If this is a strictly elemental working, stand facing the elemental quarter of your circle. In this case, the energy will be drawn through the pentagonal center of the elemental pentagram of the respective quarter, and its energy will be received through your Mercury Center, while assuming Invocation Posture.

5. Visualize your Spirit Crown Center active and open, your Kether Sphere glowing brightly just above it.

6. Begin intoning the divine names and words of your spiritual hierarchy of choice.

7. See the corresponding forces in your microcosmic sphere of sensation begin to vibrate, coming to the fore, and your sphere of sensation glowing a pulsing emerald green color.

8. When you have finished calling forth the spiritual hierarchy of Venus (or whatever planet, zodiacal sign, or element you have selected), use the Command Posture to trace the sigil of the planet and any other invocatory or geometric figures related to the planet, constellation, or element, as if inscribing it on the front portion of the outer boundary of your sphere of sensation.

9. Move or turn so that you are on the opposite side of your altar, with your back toward the quarter of the sky where the celestial body is located.

10. Visualize your sphere of sensation becoming permeable and porous, and see/feel the funnel of light forming at the Spirit Crown Point, projecting upward through the Kether Center.

11. Recite the written or chosen passage of invocation (for instance, an Orphic hymn, Hygromantic prayer, or Heptameron conjuration to the particular planet), and then powerfully vibrate the names of the hierarchies.

12. See a beam of correspondingly colored light (in our example, emerald green for Venus) shoot forth from the area of the sky housing the celestial body,

making contact with your sphere of sensation, and pouring your ætheric body through the funnel of light, powerfully charging your Middle Pillar.

13. Visualize your alchemical centers filling with the colored light and your sphere of sensation as completely radiant in it.

14. Trace a circle with your projection hand in Command Posture around the material to be consecrated, along with any invocatory figures of your own choosing.

15. Keeping the visualization of your three alchemical centers filled with colored light, the Middle Pillar glowing as planetary energy pours in through your Spirit Crown Point, and the microcosmic pathway connected, bring the energy down the Middle Pillar with an inhalation, through the Sulfur and Mercury Centers to the Salt Center. The corresponding sensations of this inpouring of energy are a full-body shudder, a surge of energy and wakefulness, a rising heartbeat, and a feeling of static electric charge on the skin, which may produce goosebumps.

16. With a powerful out-breath, see the energy surge upward from the Salt Center to the Mercury Center, using the Projection Posture to project it forward from your Mercury Center toward the implement on the altar. You may vibrate the name or word of power for the force you are projecting along with the Projection Posture. Continue this until you feel that this buildup of energy has discharged.

17. Immediately follow the last projection with the Stop Posture. Take a moment to center yourself.

18. Assume Command Posture, pointing toward the now-charged talisman, and recite your talisman's "charge." This can take the form of a brief address to the talisman, addressing it as now ensouled (loudly saying, "Creature of Venus!"), and speaking the length, purpose, and terms of its existence as a talismanic implement.

19. Take a moment to pull in more planetary energy and charge your Mercury Center. Reach the hand of projection out, palm flat over the talisman in Consecration Posture, and following the breath, visualize energy pouring from your Mercury Center through your arm and hand into the talisman.

Say, "I consecrate you a talisman of Venus." You may also choose to blow on the talisman, as this is a traditional gesture of consecration representing the enlivening of it with the breath of spirit.

20. Test the consecration by softening your gaze to examine the talisman's ætheric body. It should be glowing in either a complementary color or some variation of the colored light invoked into your sphere of sensation.

21. Wrap the talisman in black linen or silk cloth. This is essential, as this seems to seal the ætheric charge the talisman has received, preserving it from dissipation during the final banishing or warding of the space.

Directions: The Closure

1. You may at this point perform a centering rite such as the Elemental Middle Pillar, Three Centers Distillation, or Uniting Above and Below or proceed to the closing.

2. Declare the purpose for the rite accomplished and perform a final invocation of Highest Deity.

3. Perform a warding or banishing rite.

4. Declare a license to depart: for example, "I now release any and all spirits, intelligences, and other entities imprisoned by this ceremony. Depart in peace to your realms and let there be peace between us. Yet be ready to come again when you are called."

5. Record your experience, thoughts, feelings, sensations, and any other noteworthy details in your magical record.

CONCLUSION

Ritual work is an essential part of a magical practice, and the techniques and sequencing I have given exemplify the flow and form of ceremonial magic. Considerations such as astrological timing, elemental and celestial energies to be used, and the proper format for the intended ritual are all essential parts of crafting a rite. The tools I have given you should also help you to craft your own ritual, catered to your specific needs and goals. It should be kept in mind, however, that the foundation of your practice is rooted in the three alchemical centers, the Middle Pillar, and your alembic or sphere of sensation. The æther is the animating force of your magic.

CONCLUSION

Ætheric magic is a comprehensive system of magic, and this introductory work is meant to be the beginning of your personal journey on the path of a Western tradition of energy work. I sincerely hope you will return to this book time and again, since it can indeed be used as a manual for further experimentation, progress, and your own research. With this broad outline of sequential alignment in exercises and techniques, it is also hoped that the practitioner will have achieved a greater degree of fluency, power, and enjoyment in magical ritual. With diligent practice, the ætheric magic practitioner can come to further health and life by the use and command of these energies in the alchemical process of transmutation.

As I have shown, this path is indeed alchemical—in the course of this book's praxis, the practitioner has united the active and passive, resolved the salt and sulfur into the mercury, and taken a leap toward the coagulation of the alchemical Stone of the Philosophers, by assimilating the powers of the elements, planets, and stars into the little universe—the magical microcosm of the self. Yet the alchemical process is not a one-and-done deal. It is an ascending spiral of continual refinement, discovery, and wonder.

What's more—we can participate in each other's journeys and grow together. Join our community online in the Ætheric Magic group on Facebook. For further learning, sign up for the ætheric magic course, which I am offering on my website (ikebaker.com), and feel free to reach out to me with any questions by filling out the question submission form there. It has been an honor and privilege to be your teacher, and may many blessings abound in the years to come to you and yours, in magic.

GLOSSARY OF POSTURES

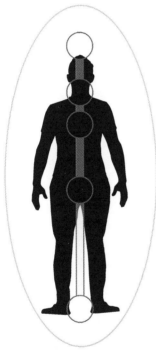

Middle Pillar Posture

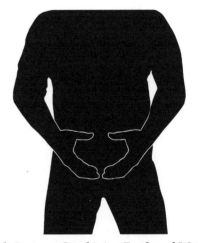

Salt Posture: Combining Earth and Water

Mercury Posture: Mediating Position

Sulfur Posture: Combining Fire and Air

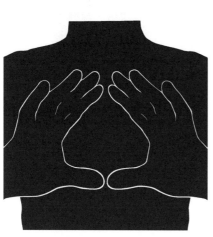

Quintessence Posture

Deity-Form Posture

Projection Posture, Step 1

Projection Posture, Step 2

Projection Posture, Step 3

Stop Posture

Command Posture

Invocation Posture

Consecration Posture

Magician (Second Arcanum) Posture

Temperance (Fourteenth Arcanum) Posture

TABLES ⊕F SYMBOLS

CORRESPONDENCES ⊕N THE TREE ⊕F LIFE

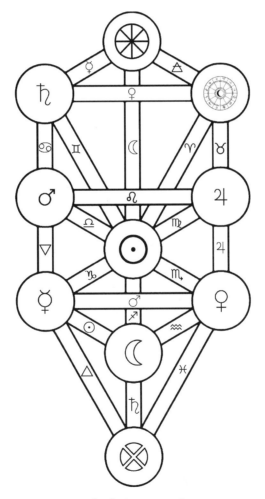

Tree of Life Correspondences

AGRIPPA'S SPIRITUAL HIERARCHIES

Divine Names	Sephirothic Names	Archangelic Names	Order of Angels	Dionysian Names	Celestial Names	Celestial Intelligences
Eheieh	Kether	Metatron	Chayoth ha Kodesh	Seraphim	Rashith ha Galgalim	
Yod Tetragrammaton	Chokmah	Raziel	Ophanim	Cherubim	Mazzaloth	
Tetragrammaton Elohim	Binah	Zaphkiel	Aralim	Thrones	Shabbathai	Agiel
El	Chesed	Zadkiel	Chasmalim	Dominations	Tzedek	Iophiel
Elohim Gibor	Geburah	Kamael	Seraphim	Powers	Ma'adim	Graphiel
Eloah	Tiphareth	Raphael	Melekhim	Virtues	Shamesh	Nakhiel
Tetragrammaton Sabaoth	Netzach	Haniel	Elohim	Principalities	Nogah	Hagiel
Elohim Sabaoth	Hod	Michael	Beni Elohim	Archangels	Kokhab	Tiriel
Shadai	Yesod	Gabriel	Cherubim	Angels	Levannah	Shelakel
Adonai Melekh	Malkuth	Meshiach	Ishim	Blessed Souls	Holomiesodoth	

DRAWING THE PENTAGRAMS AND HEXAGRAMS

Invoking pentagrams begin at a point moving *toward* the elemental arm of the pentagram. To banish, begin at the elemental point—e.g., bottom left for earth—and move *away* from the angle.

Invoking Earth

Invoking Fire

Invoking Water

Invoking Air

Banishing Earth

Banishing Fire

Banishing Water

Banishing Air

Invoking and Banishing Pentagrams

The planetary symbols can be imagined or traced in the center of the figure after the triangles of each hexagram are traced. The hexagram for the sun requires the tracing of all other planetary hexagrams as one hexagram in the following order: Saturn, Jupiter, Mars, Venus, Mercury, and Moon (see next page).

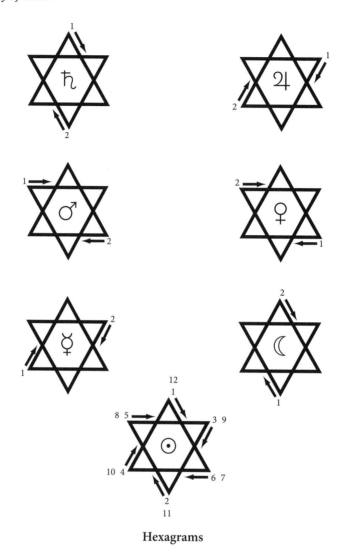

Hexagrams

HEPTAGRAM INVOCATION

Each line of the heptagram is accompanied by the vibration of a particular vowel while traced. The sequence is as follows:

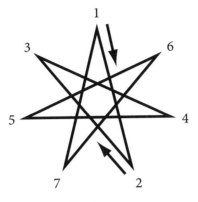

Heptagram

1. *O* as in *o*nly
2. *U* as in tr*u*e
3. *O* as in h*o*t
4. *E* as in m*ee*t
5. *A* as in c*a*re
6. *E* as in s*e*t
7. *A* as in f*a*ther

ZODIACAL COLOR CORRESPONDENCES

Glyphs	Zodiacal Sign	Tarot Trump	Color
♈	Aries	The Emperor	Red
♉	Taurus	The High Priest	Red orange
♊	Gemini	The Lovers	Orange
♋	Cancer	The Chariot	Yellow orange
♌	Leo	Strength	Yellow
♍	Virgo	The Hermit	Yellow green
♎	Libra	Justice	Green
♏	Scorpio	Death	Blue green
♐	Sagittarius	Temperance	Blue
♑	Capricorn	The Devil	Blue violet
♒	Aquarius	The Star	Violet
♓	Pisces	The Moon	Red violet

PLANETARY AND ELEMENTAL COLOR CORRESPONDENCES

Glyphs	Planet/Element	Tarot Trump	Color
♄	Saturn	The World	Black
♃	Jupiter	The Wheel of Fortune	Violet
♂	Mars	The Tower	Red
☉	Sun	The Sun	Orange
♀	Venus	The Empress	Green
☿	Mercury	The Magician	Yellow
☽	Moon	The High Priestess	Blue
△	Fire	Judgement	Red
▵	Air	The Fool	Yellow
▽	Water	The Hanged Man	Blue

Refer also to the table of correspondences of the Tree of Life on page 121.

GLOSSARY OF TERMS

Æther: The diffuse field of vibrational energy from which all other forms of energy are generated. Also used to refer to the human energy field and as a unifying term for similar concepts such as qi, prana, ki, orgone, vril, elan vital, etc.

Alchemy: A method of investigation of the underlying qualities, properties, and patterns of nature both physical and metaphysical by the application of Hermetic philosophy.

Alembic: An alchemical still used in the distillation of liquids. *See also* alchemy, ambix.

Ambix: A distillation cap or head used to collect distillate. *See also* alchemy, alembic.

Archetype: An ideal example of a certain person or thing. This initially entered the popular lexicon as a Jungian psychological concept referring to universal, inherited ideas, patterns of thought, or images present in the collective unconscious of humanity.

Assiah: The lowest of the Qabalistic Worlds, relating to physical manifestation. *See also* Qabalah, Tree of Life.

Atziluth: The highest of the Qabalistic Worlds, relating to the abstract archetypal realm preceding, and generating the process of manifestation.

Augoeidies: A Greek word meaning "luminous body." *See also* sphere of sensation.

Aura: A Vedic term for the sphere of ætheric energy surrounding an individual's physical body. *See also* sphere of sensation.

Banishing: A prophylactic ritual protocol involving the creation of both an energetically neutralized area and a container for magical workings.

Breath work: Controlled use of inhalation and exhalation as applied to energy work and meditation.

Briah: The Qabalistic World succeeding Atziluth and preceding Yetzirah, relating to the phase of manifestation that responds to the impetus of the archetypal and copies the image of an individuated idea into a workable, cognizable form, effecting the opening stages of its independent existence.

Celestial salt: The philosophic essential referring to the principle of crystallization and form in the alchemical Tria Prima. *See also* philosophical essential, Tria Prima.

Celestial sulfur: A symbolic title given in reference to the supraessential quality of activity and movement.

Channel: A distinct trajectory or pathway through which ætheric energy moves through the human body; typically used in Chinese medicine.

Chi: A term used in Chinese medicine, energy work, and energy theory denoting "breath," "vapor," "life-force energy." *See also* æther, prana.

Conjuration: A magical operation involving the calling forth of spirits for purposes of pact-making.

Dantian: A term meaning "elixir field" used in Chinese medicine and qigong to refer to centers within the human body where ætheric energy is stored as in a reservoir.

Elements: The division of matter into four distinct categories, fire, air, water, and earth, as delineated by the ancient Greek philosopher Empedocles. In later developments, a quintessence, or fifth element, of spirit is added to this. The Chinese system of elements or *wu xing* ("five phases") include fire, earth, metal, water, and wood.

Energy work: Systems of meditation, breath work, movement, and visualization aimed toward the cultivation and movement of ætheric energy in and around the physical body.

Evocation: The magical operation of calling forth entities in ceremonial ritual.

Fractal: A hypothetically infinitely repeating pattern based on mathematical number sequences.

Gnosis: A Greek word meaning "knowledge," typically in reference to concepts of perceptual experience that transcend rational thought and words.

Godform: The image associated with a particular god, usually of a classical pantheon, as envisioned in the astral (imaginal) by the mind's eye and projected into physical three-dimensional space.

Goetia: From the Greek root *goao*, meaning "to moan," and derived from the Greek word *goes*, meaning "sorcerer." A branch of Hellenistic magic that involves the conjuration of ancient Greco-Egyptian spirits, demons, and other entities for the purposes of pact-making.

Grounding: The practice of reconnecting with the physical body and mundane levels of consciousness after ritual, energy work, or another type of activity where consciousness is exalted, projected, or altered beyond its everyday qualities.

Heka: The ancient Egyptian god of magic.

Jiuziyin: The Chinese name for esoteric Taoist hand postures. *See also* mudra.

Ka: The ancient Egyptian word referring to the aspect of an individual corresponding to the ætheric body.

Ki: The Japanese term for the concept of ætheric energy. *See also* æther, chi, prana.

Macrocosm: A Greek word meaning "big cosmos," referring to the universe at large.

Mercury: The philosophical essential of the alchemical Tria Prima corresponding to the principle of the unification of opposites.

Microcosm: Meaning "small cosmos" in Greek, this term denotes the individual human in relation to the greater cosmos. *See also* macrocosm.

Monad: The highest distinct, absolute unity from which all other creation emanates. *See also* Pythagoras.

Mudra: Vedic hand postures used in pranayama and various types of yoga.

Navitoth: A Hebrew word referring to the paths on the Tree of Life. *See also* Qabalah, sephiroth, Tree of Life.

Neidan: A collection of philosophical ideas and physical, mental, and spiritual exercises composing the esoteric canon of Chinese "inner alchemy."

Pentagram: A unicursal geometric figure typified by five points, five angles, and a pentagonal central geometry.

Philosophic essentials: The three distinct essences that characterize the substratum of physical generation—salt, sulfur, and mercury—not referring to the physical materials with the same names but rather to three superessential qualities. *See also* Tria Prima.

Plane: A concept expressing a particular phase of manifestation in the divine causal chain of emanation, which exists coterminously with all other phases of the same process.

Plato: An ancient Athenian philosopher (427–348 BCE) whose dialogues featuring his teacher Socrates are the historical foundations upon which the Western esoteric traditions have been erected.

Point: A precise area where access to a specific, local region of the ætheric substructure can be gained. They are also called micro-chakras, *dines*, and *galgalim*.

Practicum: A course of practical work.

Prana: A Sanskrit word meaning "breath" and "life-force energy" used to refer to æther.

Pranayama: The movement, manipulation, and accumulation of prana in tandem with specific postures, breathing patterns, exercises, and visualizations. *See also* prana.

Protocol: A specific procedure or set of procedures.

Psyche-ætheric: Referring to the relationship between the elemental self and ætheric field of the individual. Qabalistically, the relationship between the ruach and the Nephesch. Theosophically, the relationship between the mental and astral levels with the ætheric sublevel of the physical.

Pythagoras: An ancient Greek philosopher and mathematician who approached mathematics as both a natural and metaphysical discipline and who coined the term *philosopher*.

Qabalah: A term derived from the Hebrew Q-B-L (קבל) meaning "reception." It is used to refer to a Judaic tradition of mysticism and scriptural exegesis. Other variations of spelling are *Kabbalah* and *Cabala*. However, when written with a *Q*, it typically denotes the Hermetic evolution of this form of exegesis as popularized by nineteenth- and early twentieth–century occult orders—most famously the Hermetic Order of the Golden Dawn and its offshoots.

Qi: *See* chi.

Qlipphot: In Qabalistic cosmology, originally that of Rabbi Isaac Luria and later in Hermetic Qabalistic traditions, the shells or husks of failed creation within which is trapped the divine spark. This typically refers to the averse or demonic forces that exist contiguous to and below the material world.

Quintessence: A compound word coming from the Latin *quint*, meaning "five," and *essentia*, meaning "essence"; the fifth essence or fifth element.

Rebis: A symbol of perfection in alchemy, usually rendered as a two-headed amalgam of male and female, possessing the qualities of both and uniting the powers of the sun and moon into a unified existence.

Salt: The philosophical essential of the Tria Prima of alchemy corresponding to the principle of crystallization.

Sanskrit: An ancient Indo-European language in which the scriptures of the peoples of the Indian subcontinent were written.

Sephiroth: Plural of Hebrew *sephirah,* meaning "vessel," "numeration," and "counting." These are the spheres on the Qabalistic glyph of the Tree of Life.

Sphere of sensation: A Western term for the aura. Inclusive of the entirety of the energetic and physical bodies.

Sulfur: The philosophic essential of the Tria Prima of alchemy corresponding to the principles of movement, expansion, and volatility.

Supernal: A term expressing a distinctly celestial nature, used to refer to the uppermost sephiroth of the Qabalistic Tree of Life: Kether, Chokmah, and Binah. *See also* Qabalah, sephiroth.

Tetraktys: An equilateral triangle formed by the arrangement of the numbers one through ten, arranged vertically in four horizontal rows. It is known to have a been a sacred symbol to the Pythagoreans. *See also* Pythagoras.

Theosophy: Used here to denote the philosophy, esoteric cosmology, and worldview developed by the founders of the Theosophical Society of the late 1800s to the mid-1900s.

Theurgy: A systematic technique of spiritual ascent leading to gnosis or divine union, informed principally by the Neoplatonic philosophy and metaphysical cosmology of philosophers of late antiquity, such as Iamblichus, Porphyry, Plotinus, and Proclus. *See also* gnosis.

Tree of Life: A lineal glyph or composite Qabalistic diagram illustrating a symbolic representation of the inherent pattern upon which all creation is based. It comprises spheres (*sephiroth*) and lines or paths (*netivoth*) that exist in spatial geometric relationships to one another, forming a complex whole, upon which every time of force, form, essence, and experience can be classified, and corresponded.

Tria Prima: The alchemical philosophic essentials of salt, sulfur, and mercury. *See also* philosophic essentials.

Vibration: A magical technique of intoning a divine name or word of power, utilizing diaphragmatic breathing in a way similar to singing, as the tones are bellowed powerfully and musically. In the case of the divine names of the Middle Pillar and Tree of Life visualizations, the sephiroth can be vibrated at varying pitches, from ascending to descending, to effect a corresponding sensation in the anatomical region associated with each sephirah.

Western Esoteric Traditions: A term referring to the overarching bodies of philosophy, metaphysics, and premodern science historically associated with the ancient civilizations of Iran, Egypt, and Greece, as evolved and transmitted through late antiquity, the Middle Ages, and the Renaissance, and their applications in modern times. These include astrology, alchemy, Hermeticism, magic, the tarot, angelology, Rosicrucianism, theosophy, and Freemasonry.

Yetzirah: The third Qabalistic world of "formation." This corresponds to the astral plane and astral-ætheric subplane. This level of creative manifestation from the Divine is thought of as the blueprint of material reality.

BIBLIOGRAPHY

Agrippa, Heinrich Cornelius. *Three Books of Occult Philosophy*. Book 1. Translated by Eric Purdue. Rochester, VT: Inner Traditions, 2021.

Besant, Annie, and Charles W. Leadbeater. *Thought-Forms*. London: Theosophical Publishing Society, 1905.

Bulwer-Lytton, Edward. *The Coming Race*. New York: Henry L. Hinton, 1873.

David, Rosalie. *Religion and Magic in Ancient Egypt*. London: Penguin Books, 2002.

DeMeo, James. *The Orgone Accumulator Handbook*. Ashland, OR: Natural Energy Works, 1989.

Ficino, Marsilio. *Three Books on Life*. Book 3. Edited and translated by Carol V. Kaske and John R. Clark. Binghamton, NY: Medieval & Renaissance Texts & Studies and the Renaissance Society of America, 1989.

Grimes, Shannon. *Becoming Gold: Zosimos of Panopolis and the Alchemical Arts in Roman Egypt*. Auckland: Rubedo Press, 2018.

Hall, Manly P. *The Secret Teachings of All Ages: An Encyclopedic Outline of Masonic, Hermetic, Qabbalistic and Rosicrucian Symbolical Philosophy*. San Francisco: H. S. Crocker, 1928. Electronic reproduction by J. B. Hare, Internet Sacred Texts Archive, 2001.

Hauck, Dennis. *The Complete Idiot's Guide to Alchemy: The Magic and Mystery of the Ancient Craft Revealed for Today*. New York: Penguin Books, 2008.

Kilner, John W. *The Human Atmosphere: or, The Aura Made Visible by the Aid of Chemical Screens*. New York: Rebman Company, 1911.

Leadbeater, Charles W. *Man Visible and Invisible*. London: The Theosophical Publishing House, 1964.

Lévi, Éliphas. *Transcendental Magic: Its Doctrine and Ritual.* Translated by Arthur Edward Waite. Chicago: De Laurence & Scott, 1910.

———. *The Science of Hermes.* Translated by Joseph Bouleur. Sequim, WA: Holmes Publishing Group, 2007.

McCarthy, Josephine. *Quareia Apprentice.* UK: Quareia Publishing, 2016.

Mesmer, Franz Anton. *Mesmerism: The Discovery of Animal Magnetism.* Translated by V. R. Meyers. Boulder, CO: Soul Care Publishing, 2016.

O'Neill, John. *Prodigal Genius: Biography of Nikola Tesla.* Long Island, NY: 1944. Reprint, Albuquerque, NM: Brotherhood of Life, 1994.

Plato. *The Complete Works of Plato.* Edited by John M. Cooper. Indianapolis: Hackett Publishing, 1997.

———. *The Timaeus of Plato.* Translated by R. D. Archer-Hind. New York: MacMillan & Co., 1888.

Porphyry of Tyre. *Select Works of Porphyry.* Gloucestershire, UK: The Prometheus Trust, 1999.

Powell, Arthur Edward. *The Etheric Double: The Heath Aura of Man.* Wheaton, IL: Quest Books, 1969.

Prasad, Rama. *Nature's Finer Forces.* Adyar, India: Theosophical Publishing House, 1947.

Rankine, David. *The Grimoire Encyclopaedia.* Vol. 1. West Yorkshire, UK: Hadean Press, 2023.

Scarborough, Samuel. "The Lesser Ritual of the Pentagram." In *The Light Extended: A Journal of the Golden Dawn.* Vol. 1. Edited by Frater Yechidah. Dublin: Kerubim Press, 2019.

Shaw, Gregory. *Theurgy and the Soul: The Neoplatonism of Iamblichus.* 2nd ed. Kettering, OH: Angelico Press, 2014.

Teiser, Steven F. *The Ghost Festival in Medieval China.* Princeton, NJ: Princeton University Press, 1988.

Waisberg, Ethan, Joshua Ong, Mouayad Masalkhi, and Andrew G. Lee. "Near Infrared/Red Light Therapy a Potential Countermeasure for Mitochondrial Dysfunction in

Spaceflight Associated Neuro-Ocular Syndrome (SANS)." *Eye* 38, no. 13 (2024): 2499–501. doi:10.1038/s41433-024-03091-4.

Wen, Benebell. *The Tao of Craft: Fu Talismans and Casting Sigils in the Eastern Esoteric Tradition*. Berkeley, CA: North Atlantic Books, 2016.

TO WRITE TO THE AUTHOR

If you wish to contact the author or would like more information about this book, please write to the author in care of Llewellyn Worldwide Ltd. and we will forward your request. Both the author and publisher appreciate hearing from you and learning of your enjoyment of this book and how it has helped you. Llewellyn Worldwide Ltd. cannot guarantee that every letter written to the author can be answered, but all will be forwarded. Please write to:

Ike Baker
℅ Llewellyn Worldwide
2143 Wooddale Drive
Woodbury, MN 55125-2989
Please enclose a self-addressed stamped envelope for reply,
or $1.00 to cover costs. If outside the U.S.A., enclose
an international postal reply coupon.

Many of Llewellyn's authors have websites with additional information and resources. For more information, please visit our website at http://www.llewellyn.com.